Erik Hagen was born in the UK to Norwegian parents. The family came to Western Australia in his childhood and he has been there ever since.

He came late to medicine but has now been in that field for over 40 years.

He has had a career including country general practice, retrieval medicine with the Royal Flying Doctor Service of Australia and working in hospital emergency departments. He has been involved in his hobby of motor sport medicine, including Formula 1 and World Rallying for the last 30 years.

To all those that care for others, whether professional, amateur, volunteer, paid or unpaid…thank you.

My stories are your stories too.

Erik Hagen

IMPERFECT RECOLLECTIONS

Memory fragments from an ageing medico

AUSTIN MACAULEY PUBLISHERS™

LONDON • CAMBRIDGE • NEW YORK • SHARJAH

ISBN 9781528991360 (Paperback)
ISBN 9781528991377 (Hardback)
ISBN 9781528991391 (ePub e-book)

www.austinmacauley.com

First Published (2020)
Austin Macauley Publishers Ltd
25 Canada Square
Canary Wharf
London
E14 5LQ

There are many people to thank.

Arthur Pate, who gave me a love of words and language and taught me to spread them thickly on the toast of life.

Many friends and colleagues, who were kind enough to read some or all of the stories and offer me advice and encouragement. In particular, Steve Dunjey, Lachy McTaggart, Mike Lefroy, Rob Gillett, Don Degiglio and Frank Sheehan.

And, to all my family for their love and encouragement; to my dear wife Dimity, who laughed, loved and cried with me and supported me during so many of these experiences and who is sadly no longer with us; and to my Margie, who with love and patience, held my hand during this book's long gestation.

Introduction

Albert Facey wrote a book called *A Fortunate Life*. Some of you may remember it. He had a life full of trials and hardship but indeed created a fortunate life for himself despite adversity.

I too have had 'a fortunate life' but most would agree that I really have been fortunate and had relatively little in the way of adversity, enough to blight me on occasions, but most of the time things have worked out pretty well for me.

It was relatively easy for me. I was born into the upper middle class, had a good education at a private school and then went onto university with nary a thought or indeed a check in my ordained progress.

I absolutely know that I have been incredibly fortunate, far more than many others and perhaps more than I deserve (Well, I think I am thoroughly deserving anyway – but then, doesn't everybody?).

What is so important is that every child in our country should, or rather must, have the opportunities that I have had. We should also be creating the best possible environment for them so they can pick up their particular baton and run with it as far as they want to go.

Medicine was my second university degree, a slow starter, perhaps. Now, I have been in the medical field for over forty years.

Being a doctor is a unique privilege. One can get close to people, usually stripped of all artifice and sometimes, if you are lucky, really help them and best of all, occasionally help them to live when they should have died.

My patients have let me into their lives and for that I am eternally grateful.

In my professional life, I have spent time as a country GP, a flying doctor in the RFDS, worked in a metropolitan Emergency Department and spent plenty of my time in my hobby of motor sport medicine especially in the fields of Formula 1 and World Rallying.

I have had a bloody great time!

This book is a collection of stories that have either happened to me or I have observed over that forty-plus year period.

The stories are true and happened largely as I have described them. The names are not.

Many people will undoubtedly think that they recognise themselves or others in them. I am here to tell you that you are RIGHT but that you are also WRONG. What you are recognising is the human condition with all its heroism and foibles that exists within all of us.

There is humour but also pathos in everyone. Humour helps us cope with the pathos. As we know it has been often said:

If you don't laugh, you weep.

It's okay to do both.

I hope you enjoy them. I enjoyed writing them but most of all I have enjoyed the privilege of being allowed to get close to so many wonderful people during my professional life.

"To **cure**…sometimes, to **relieve**…often and to **comfort**…always."

– Hippocrates

"No man is an island, entire of itself; every man is a piece of the continent, a part of the main, any man's death diminishes me, because I am involved in mankind; and therefore, never send to know for whom the bell tolls; it tolls for thee."

– John Donne

Author's Note
(A Note from Me!)

I have tried to write these stories as if you and I, perhaps old friends, are sitting down to share a cup of tea, coffee or something stronger. With a bit of time to kill, I might perchance tell you an amusing tale or two.

Many of these are just a narrative, whereas others need some medical explanation to enable the context of the story to become clear.

Some stories, such as the ones about asthma and the heart, require more medical illumination to make them sensible. I have attempted to keep that to a minimum and simplify things so that even I can understand them, without losing meaning.

So, if some stories carry on a bit too much about medical stuff, please forgive me.

My wife says that I can be a bit pedantic!

Muriel

MURIEL was about thirty when I first met her. She lived in a small town a few kilometres away from ours, and which had shrunk in size and importance with the decline of the local industry. As a result of this shrinkage, there were a lot of spare houses which were then used for social housing. More unkind people than myself have described this place as the last refuge for the genetically fatigued.

Anyway, back to Muriel. She was a large, unkempt woman who shambled about town. She smoked incessantly and had appalling teeth. Her IQ was well below triple figures. Once, in her youth, she had been slightly attractive and as a result used to be raffled off at the local pub to the highest bidder after football on Saturday night.

As the years progressed, the ticket price dropped and eventually she slipped from first to third prize. She didn't seem to mind that, accepting it with the same somewhat bovine countenance she habitually displayed to the world.

She lived at the only boarding house in the town – a ramshackle wooden building on stilts (which later burnt down) run by the Jones family whose IQ was only marginally above Muriel's. The young Jones children used to tease her unmercifully and occasionally throw stones.

I hope you are getting the picture of a lost soul because that is what she was. At some stage she had been briefly married and had a child who she had given up for adoption. She would sometimes speak wistfully about the child and have elaborate ideas about going to visit him but she never did.

She also used to smoke a bit of 'loco' weed (marijuana), which used to make her psychotic. It usually meant a trip to the metropolitan psychiatric hospital for in-patient treatment. She liked it there and was always sad when they tossed her out after a few days. Almost every time I saw her in the surgery in her town, she would ask to be sent back there and on occasions would get quite sulky when I refused.

The tale, which I wanted to share with you, relates to her psychotic episodes.

The psychiatric hospital had quite properly put her on an injectable (depot) anti-psychotic medication called Modecate. This meant, instead of relying on the patient to take daily oral medication, they just have a monthly injection. Generally, this practice is now frowned upon as it is felt in these days of political correctness that the patient doesn't have a 'stake' in their treatment.

Since Muriel's case, like so many others, was characterised by a total lack of insight into her condition. I really didn't have a problem with that because this system actually worked and kept her on some semblance of an even keel. The only trouble is that one of the side effects was that she used to chew her tongue a bit but I guess you can't have everything.

In the late 1980s, prescription drugs for pensioners were free but this changed to impose a modest fee of $2.50 per script for Health Care Card holders. Muriel never had any money on her (but always miraculously had enough to buy smokes!). So, for about a year, we (the surgery) would buy her Modecate and continue with the monthly injections.

One day I had had enough and, in retrospect foolishly, refused to buy any more injections for her. We warned her about the impending leap into self-responsibility for a number of weeks. Alas, to no avail!

The day came that she rolled up at our branch surgery in her small town which was a nice timber building in the grounds of the local hospital. Muriel wanted her injection and there wasn't one. I almost wavered because she looked so forlorn but I held firm, telling her that all she had to do was give us $2.50 and we would do the rest. She had a tear in the eye and the expression was even more mulish than normal.

The tongue chewing accelerated to a blur. Muttering to herself she finally shuffled dejectedly away.

I, prissy idiot that I am, was saddened but pleased that I had been 'firm but fair' and that Muriel was at last on the road to self-determination.

That night she burnt the branch surgery down.

Muriel's trial was set down for the local District Court and of course yours truly was one of the star witnesses for the prosecution. I had never been to court before and had a fairly even mixture of interest and terror in the proceedings.

I was sitting outside the court, as all witnesses have to do before being called doing the usual things, scratching my leg, staring at the wall etc. Then, "Call Dr…Call Dr…" repeated by a couple of minions and I was on.

As I was escorted into the courtroom, Muriel who was sitting at the defence table caught sight of me. "Hallo, Doctor…" she yelled a couple of times.

"Oh, God!" I averted my head, held the hand nearest to her up to shield my face and scuttled in a most undignified fashion into the witness box where I was duly sworn in with dear old idiotic Muriel beaming up at me and giving the occasional wave to ensure I noticed her from the body of the court.

I gave most of my evidence, which was quite straightforward and largely was the tale I have told so far. At the end, the judge leaned forward and said, "How would you sum up Muriel?" To which I replied:

"She is overweight, smokes too much, has appalling dentition, lives in terrible social circumstances, has a borderline IQ and has absolutely no prospects for improvement in the future."

After giving evidence any witness is allowed to sit in the court and watch the proceedings from there on in.

Which, I did.

Unfortunately, one of the only free seats was directly behind the defence table. Muriel turned around and gave me a big smile and said:

"Thanks for putting in a good word for me!"

It took me a couple of minutes to regain my composure.

A little while later, the taped police interview was played which I watched with great interest. Right at the end she burst into tears, which made everyone a bit sad until she wailed to her interrogator:

"It's not fair. Every time Janet (see Janet – Muscle Car Lady) goes mad, Dr sends her to mad hospital, but every time I go mad, he sends me to jail!"

The police prosecutor turned around to look at me, shook his head and clucked his tongue disapprovingly. Again, I needed a little time to compose myself.

Muriel was found not guilty on the grounds of diminished responsibility and is currently languishing at Her Majesty's pleasure, where she always wanted to be, in the main psychiatric hospital. I think that she is still there.

But, I Love Him

Our small country town was at the foot of an escarpment, in which were a number of dams to provide domestic water and farm irrigation for those properties 'down on the flats'.

As the name 'flats' suggest, the land was quite flat! This lent itself to flood irrigation, called 'border-dyke' irrigation, where lengths of paddock were punctuated every 100 metres or so by small earthworks or dykes. This enabled the water to cover the ground better, being held into a confined area between the 'dykes' rather than just flooding willy-nilly over the land.

When I told him the name of the type of irrigation, a rather dim, homophobic acquaintance of mine thought I was referring to a female customs official (sorry about that one!).

While irrigation was great in the summer months, the 'flats' were inevitably waterlogged and soggy, frequently with ankle-deep water, during winter.

Over time, the farm holdings had increased in size and as a result many farms had the odd cottage on them, no longer required for the farmer's family, which were rented out.

Jane came to town, a few years after I arrived, with her partner (I never knew his name). They were both not working and on the Unemployment Benefit. They used to drink a bit (especially him) and occasionally smoke dope when they could both get some and afford it.

They rented one of the cottages I was talking about 'down on the flats'.

Jane used to come and see me for various things at the surgery. She was always shy and diffident. She had been quite pretty but somewhere along the line she had lost several of her teeth and the ridge of her brows was quite thickened. This was due to scar tissue and to me is a tell-tale sign that she had been bashed. Often. She had some other scars on her face and one large one, which distorted her lower lip.

She looked and acted like someone who had been the victim of prolonged domestic violence.

Sometimes I would gently ask her about her home life and relationship but each time she would avow that everything was fine. I felt quite helpless.

One winter's evening, after we had been having heavy rain for a few days and the 'flats' were well and truly waterlogged, I received a phone call from the hospital just when I was thinking of going to my nice warm bed.

Jane had come in a quite a state – crying and incoherent.

I went to the hospital and she was almost hysterical. I gave her a small sedative to alleviate her distress and this is the story she told me.

She and her partner had been at home and had a few drinks in front of the open fire. He had had a lot more to drink than she had, an argument (she said over nothing) had developed; he had started to hit her around the head with his fists (like he probably had many times before).

To escape him, she had locked herself in the lavatory, which was outside on the back veranda. This had enraged him and he had tried to open the door to no avail. He then went and got the axe from the wood heap and started to chop at the lavatory door, all the while shouting abuse and threatening violent retribution when he finally got to her.

Terrified, she managed to remove the louvered glass from the loo window and squeeze herself out of the small aperture without him realising. She had then run ankle-deep through the flooded paddock to the next-door neighbour's house who kindly took her to the hospital.

She was dressed only in her nightgown and Ugg boots. She was freezing cold, wet and splattered with mud. She had a badly grazed knee where she had fallen during her flight. I examined her and made sure there were no other injuries apart from the knee, and then arranged to admit her, under my bed-card, to the hospital overnight. I wrote her up for sedation on the medication chart.

The lovely nursing staff looked after her like one of their own. She had a nice hot shower, a change of clothing and a meal. They cleaned and dressed her knee. They then tucked her up in bed and thankfully she was able to get to sleep with the help of the sleeping tablet.

The hospital was always locked up at night. We were fairly sure that her partner didn't know where she was (apparently, he was too far gone to realise she wasn't there until the next morning) and also rang the police to tell them what had happened. They kindly said that they would patrol past the hospital several times overnight to make sure all was well.

The next day when I saw her on the usual ward round, she had settled down a lot but was still terrified as to what her partner would do to her, if and, when they were reunited.

What to do?

Jane and I had a long discussion as to what her options were. She vehemently stated that she was not going back to him and that she wanted a clean break. I suggested temporary accommodation at a refuge out of town.

We had no shelters of any kind in our small town (to have her still in town may well have been a problem as nothing stays secret for long). The nearby regional town had a good women's shelter run by a friend of mine. Far away enough to make it difficult for her partner to trace. We arranged for Jane to go down there later that day. One of the nursing staff, who lived in that direction, very sweetly gave her a lift when her shift at our hospital finished that afternoon.

That was that. A good deed done, and Jane safely out of the clutches of her abusive partner.

I was absolutely gobsmacked, later in the week, to see them both driving down the main street in town, outwardly happy, cuddling up on the front seat of his car and looking like butter wouldn't melt in their mouths!

She came to see me the next week and I asked what had happened and why she had 'gone back to him'.

Her answer floored me – "But, I love him!"

How sad is that. This poor woman had been reduced to such a dependency, that this bastard could do what he liked to her, knowing that she would always come crawling back.

To me, domestic violence is all about the inadequacies, and the self-perceived powerlessness, of the perpetrator and his (or her) need to exercise control and power over someone else whom they perceive to be vulnerable and therefore, less powerful than themselves. Rarely is it exclusively sexual though some of the abuse may take that form. The sad thing is, often the recipient is so bowed by this that they are unable to break free and indeed take most, if not all, of the blame for 'upsetting' him (or her).

It is heart-wrenching to see the appalling loss of another human being's inherent personal dignity. All for some low life to enjoy a power trip.

In its basest form, domestic violence is physical but it may take many forms including emotional and verbal abuse and financial control and manipulation. A similar type of 'violence' also exists in the work place where it is called bullying.

In fact, abusers of any sort, domestic or otherwise, are indeed inadequate bullies and must be called out for what they are at every opportunity and in every possible way.

Who amongst us can honestly say they have never been bullied? I have been.

Euthanasia

Euthanasia has always been a difficult and thorny question, which has polarised society over the ages.

Opinions vary from the concept that all life is sacred and should therefore be preserved at all costs, regardless of the misery of the individual concerned, to – "…you wouldn't treat a dog that badly." So, why prolong a life of needless suffering, when there is no hope that the condition will improve?

Some even go so far as to say that healthy but 'bad' people should be euthanised for their crimes as seen in the supporters of the death penalty. Of course, that would only apply to low lives such as rapists, child molesters and drug dealers and never to good, decent people like us. It would happen to 'other families' and never to ours.

Euthanasia has been illegal in Australia. Many state parliaments are currently debating that question and Voluntary Assisted Dying legislation has been passed already in one or two states. In some European jurisdictions also it is now legal and there are some anecdotal stories of the system being abused.

"*Quis custodiet ipsos custodes*?" – "Who will guard the guardians themselves?" One only has to look at Germany in the 1930s and 1940s to see how that system can get out of hand.

Doctors are often on the horns of a dilemma. A patient with a terminal illness, in severe intractable pain and requiring more and more pain relief, which seems to barely do anything. What do you do?

Over the years it is not unknown for the narcotic dose to be gradually increased or simple treatments such as antibiotics for an infective condition to be withheld, knowing that these actions will hasten death. A number of doctors have faced court in the past for such 'sins' of omission or commission.

I don't know what the answer is, but here is a tale.

Jonathan Smythe was a really nice person, a good husband and father and a well-respected member of the community.

He had a lovely way of looking you straight in the eye, shaking your hand firmly and asking how you and your family were. He was quietly spoken but had a great sense of humour that would emerge when you least expected it.

I had known him for a good few years and he used to attend the surgery to have his blood pressure checked and his prescriptions renewed.

On this day he came in to see me, again to have his blood pressure checked and get a new prescription for his tablets.

Almost as an afterthought he pointed to his right upper arm and said, "I've got the twitches, Doc. It sometimes keeps me awake at night."

Upon examination, his right biceps muscle was indeed 'twitching', called fasciculation in medical terms. There could be a number of reasons for this; some of them not so bad and some of them very bad.

I did some basic blood tests, which were all negative and then sent him for nerve conduction studies and a muscle biopsy.

The results showed that he had motor neurone disease – a dreadful diagnosis.

I don't know how much you know about it but it is very unpleasant and invariably fatal. A number of famous people such as David Niven and Dudley Moore have suffered and died from it.

Forgive me for quoting Wikipedia but they have this to say about it:

A motor neuron disease (MND) is any of five neurological disorders that selectively affect motor neurons, the cells that control voluntary muscle activity including speaking, walking, swallowing and general movement of the body. They are neurodegenerative in nature, and cause increasing disability and eventually, death.

The patient becomes increasingly weak, with difficulty carrying out the normal routines of daily living – can't speak, can't swallow, can't eat and eventually can't breathe. The appalling thing is that their thought processes and mental faculties remain intact and there is no diminution of their mental capacity. At least in some cases of dementia, whoever controls these things has the decency to allow the person to become unaware of what is happening to them – not so MND.

The final refinement of the torture is that those motor neurons that are still functioning, fire off at odd intervals giving the sufferer the added torment of severe and agonising muscle spasms.

Jon and his wife, Anne, came to see me after they had had the follow-up appointment I had arranged with a neurologist. They were aware of the diagnosis and its eventual outcome.

Anne understandably was quite tearful, and Jon seemed to be more stoical, greeting me with the usual look in the eye, firm handshake and enquiry after my family.

We talked a little about the diagnosis and what it meant. (I confess, I had to do some reading up on the subject, as it is not a diagnosis, thankfully, that I see often in my patients.)

At the end of the consultation Jon again looked me in the eye and said:

"I understand it can get pretty bad toward the end?" I agreed.

"You will look after me at the end, won't you, Doc? You know what I mean?"

I said I would and we left it at that.

Over the next two years, Jon's condition gradually declined. He stopped work and he and Anne took a number of holidays, which they both loved. They would come and show me the photos. I felt ghastly.

The time came when Jon and Anne weren't coping at home any more. Jon was essentially bed-bound, couldn't toilet himself, had increasing difficulty eating and drinking, breathing was a bit laboured and the muscle spasms were becoming intolerable.

We admitted him to a private ward in the local hospital.

We gave him intravenous fluids and diazepam and morphine for the muscle spasms.

One day, on the morning ward round, I went to his room. Anne was with him.

He said (with difficulty), "I've had enough, Doc. It's time to help me out like you promised."

Anne said, "It's time, Doc. Please help him."

Here was someone whom I liked and respected, dying slowly, in agony, an undignified death.

What would you do?

Leaving aside any moral questions, killing someone is relatively easy. It can be done by injecting (via the drip), high dose morphine and when the patient becomes unconscious, injecting a large amount of intravenous potassium chloride which stops the heart instantly.

Jon died peacefully with his beloved Anne by his side. No one in the family has ever spoken about what happened and neither have I until now.

Just a pertinent postscript:

Years later I had occasion to be involved, by invitation, in a panel discussion about euthanasia at the ethics centre of my son's school. The moderator was a priest, a fantastic person who makes people think that if he believes, there just might be something in this religion thing.

There were some quite strong practising Christians in the group, some of whom came out quite vehemently against euthanasia. Interestingly, everyone agreed that in the case of MND this was the one exception to the rule. Easy to talk about over a wine or in a panel but different when one is at the pointy end.

I thought to myself that you are either against it or for it. It is either morally right or it is wrong and you can't 'have two bob each way' – that's what I thought.

So, I smiled politely and said nothing.

Janet, the 'Muscle Car Lady'

Janet was an interesting gal.

She lived in a small town, slowly dying (the town that is, not Janet!), a few kilometres away from our town.

I always used to think of her as 'The Muscle Car Lady'.

This was because she drove a complete beast of a car, with a somewhat startling paint job and the words, 'Muscle Car' (for some reason entwined with vine leaves) on the driver's door. The car itself made a very deep-throated burble as she drove it around town, much to the admiration of some of the locals.

She bought it after a particularly lucrative stint working 'on the game', as a prostitute in a mining town many hours' drive inland from the coast. She would occasionally disappear from her usual abode for anything up to a few weeks to top up her bank account in this manner.

Physically, she was a little unprepossessing. She had a pleasant enough face, though one would not have called her beautiful and she was somewhat overweight without being morbidly obese. She used to wear, what I thought was faintly inappropriate, girlish, coquettish clothes, from which she used to bulge at odd places – bit like an overfilled sack. She had spindly legs and often used to totter about on impossibly high-heeled stiletto shoes. How she ever drove the 'Muscle Car' with that footwear was a mystery to me. Oh, I forgot to mention the often laddered, flesh bulging, fishnet stockings that she frequently sported.

Coupled with a feather boa, she was a sight to behold and obviously every lusty miner's dream!

Janet came to my attention, not because of her moneymaking enterprises or her choice of car, but rather because of her penchant for smoking, on occasions only, marijuana and then entering into psychotic and delusional behaviour.

Besides that she would come into our branch surgery to see me for various reasons like the 'pill' etc. She would totter in the door on her heels, bulging alarmingly and fluttering impossibly long false eyelashes at all and sundry and trailing the feather boa. In the waiting room, the young local girls would giggle admiringly, whereas the older matrons would mutter darkly amongst themselves.

But I digress. Back to the loco weed.

There were two occasions that stay in my mind. The first was what I think of as 'the clothesline' and the second 'the hospital' incident.

The Clothesline

I used to go up to the branch surgery in her town twice a week on an afternoon and run a GP clinic for the locals.

On this occasion, I was working through the day's list of mainly minor problems, with a few major ones thrown in, when the secretary called me out of my consulting room to take a phone call.

It was the police and could I please go to Janet's house as she had apparently gone mad, tied herself to the backyard clothesline and was shouting abuse at anyone who came near her.

I apologised to the waiting patients, jumped in my car and drove the short distance to Janet's house. By the time I got there, a light rain was falling.

Around the back of the house I found a police officer plus two of the local ambulance people sheltering from the increasing rain under the back veranda, looking, in a somewhat astonished manner, at Janet tied to the clothesline.

She was sitting with her back against the upright pole of the Hills Hoist with her legs splayed out in front of her. She was dressed in a quite flimsy nightdress and dressing gown, or should I say *peignoir*? Her rather straggly, scant hair was plastered to her head by the drizzle. She was bulging a bit.

As I approached, she looked up at me with a brilliant smile and as I crouched alongside her, she solemnly informed me that she was the Virgin Mary and that the birth of the infant Jesus was imminent.

With that, she commenced to puff and pant at a tremendous rate, occasionally break off to strain, with an increasingly puce face. The acrid smell of faeces indicated to me that at least she had been able to push something out!

I became quite alarmed and lent forward to restrain her. At that instant she screamed, "Help me, help me, my water has broken," and clutching me close, pissed into my right shoe.

Those police and ambulance bastards nearly wet themselves also.

Anyway, with that she subsided somewhat and listened to my pleas that the 'baby' should be delivered in more salubrious surrounds and allowed herself to be assisted to the waiting ambulance with me squelching in my inundated shoe behind.

After suitable sedation and certification she was transferred to the metropolitan mental health facility.

It took a lot of work to get my shoe to take a shine again.

The Hospital

The hospital incident occurred a few months later after her release from the mental health facility and after she had been home for a while. Again the dreaded dope was the cause.

She came to see me one afternoon in the branch surgery and seemed to be acting a little oddly. She was into a religious theme with emphasis on redemption and the coming apocalypse. While that in itself was not reason for alarm, in fact lots of supposedly sane people carry on like that, she was looking quite wild-eyed and ranting a bit. There was a bit of foamy spittle at one corner of her mouth.

After some discussion, mainly her raving and me listening, she agreed that she should come to hospital for a bit of a rest, dressed up as a quasi-religious retreat.

Off she went to the local hospital and, after consultation with her psychiatrist and the use of some sedatives, it was agreed to allow her to settle down there and get the weed out of her system, rather than undertake the longish journey to the metropolitan mental health facility at that time.

For a day or so, the plan seemed to be working and Janet was displaying all the attributes of a model patient. You know the ones – do as you are told, take the medicine, eat the food, don't abuse the staff and above all don't ask any embarrassing questions to which I don't know the answer.

Then disaster struck.

The hospital rang me at home at about 9 p.m. one night saying that Janet had gone loopy (the nurse's words, not mine) and had attempted to take a new-born baby from her cot in the maternity section.

Apparently, what had happened was that it was visiting hours and the new mum was showing her brand new, lovely baby to her family, which included her husband, his brother and her father.

Janet had appeared in the doorway and gone to the cot and started to lift the baby out. What amazed me was that none of the male relatives present had done a thing – they just looked at her dumbly. Mum however, saved the day. With all the fierceness of a lioness protecting her cub, she launched herself at Janet, wrested the-now-squalling infant from her grasp and landed a terrific slap on her nose.

When I arrived Janet had been restrained by the staff in an empty room and some sedation given by injection.

She was a sad and sorry sight, sitting dejectedly on her bed, weeping silently with a mixture of tears and snot, mixed with a little blood, running down her face.

She was making no attempt to wipe it away but rather gave an occasional wet sniff, which achieved little. It really was heart-wrenching to see.

Mental illness is often awful and is always sad.

It was time to commit her to the metropolitan mental health facility, as we were clearly unable to control and treat her where she was. I wrote out the necessary forms and arranged for the ambulance to attend for the journey to Perth.

By the time the ambulance arrived, Janet had gone into what I can only describe as a manic phase.

She was loudly proclaiming the arrival of the day of reckoning and urging all around her to repent and embrace the Lord.

She agreed to accompany us (myself and one of the ambulance officers) to the ambulance, which was at the Emergency entrance, down a few corridors, on the other side of the hospital.

At that time of night (by now about 11 p.m.), the night lights were on and the corridors were lit by a series of ceiling down lights, rather dim. Looking down the corridors there were pools of light separated by areas of darkness.

Janet took one look down the corridor and promptly refused to go, stating the Lord was the light and the Devil was in the darkness. I convinced her that we should run between the pools of light, and myself and the ambulance officer – one either side of her – would protect her from the Devil lurking in the shadows.

We must have presented an odd sight. A concerted rush, reminiscent of a rugby scrum (or more correctly a loose maul), past the shadows and a prolonged pause under each downlight where the Lord was praised and the saints blessed for protecting her during the passage through the preceding darkness.

It was quite exhausting and I am ashamed to say that by the time we reached the ambulance, both the ambulance guy and myself were quivering with barely suppressed mirth.

As we got to the back door of the ambulance, a light rain was falling (it rains a lot there.).

We helped Janet up into the back of the ambulance and at that moment she turned around, spread her arms wide and leaning at an angle of about forty-five degrees out of the back, loudly began to extol the coming of the Lord.

This had all the elements of a black farce.

The ambulance guy and I were supporting her to stop her falling and at this stage the suppressed mirth – really tension – exploded and we both laughed hysterically.

We dropped her.

Fortunately, we all fell in a tangle of bodies and limbs onto the wet tarmac and no one was injured. That seemed to subdue Janet and she was assisted to the ambulance stretcher, further sedation given and they made an uneventful journey to the metropolitan area.

Janet made a good recovery and came back to her town, swearing off the weed. She had occasional relapses but never of the scale of the two previous episodes.

She bought a property a little way out of her town and started to breed horses, which she turned out to be very good at.

Sadly, a highway realignment engulfed her small farm and she subsequently left the district.

I have not seen her since.

Be Careful of What You Say

When you are a doctor in a small town, whether you like it or not, you are an important part of the fabric of that society and generally considered by most to be towards the top of the social and community hierarchy.

I went to practise medicine in such a place and initially thought nothing of it. I threw myself into an extremely interesting and varied job.

It took me a while to remember patients' names, even after I had met and treated them for some time (I'm hopeless like that.).

I would dread going to the supermarket, as I would be greeted with a cheery, "G'day, Doc, what were the results of my blood test?" I would stare at them blankly, only having a vague notion of who they were.

I resorted to that wonderful phrase made famous by Doc Martin in the TV show of the same name – *Make an Appointment!* I knew how he felt.

As the years went on, I gradually got to know most, if not all, of my patients and where each individual and family fitted into the general scheme of things. I could quite happily converse with them outside of the surgery, enquire after their health and relay test results without turning a hair.

The first inkling of my supposed standing in the community was again in the supermarket, when in a friendly way people would examine the contents of my shopping trolley and ask if a particular product was any good. Sometimes I would see them scuttle off to the appropriate aisle to get some for themselves! Occasionally, I would get feedback at the next surgery visit as to whether they liked it or not!

I would sometimes be stopped in the street and be asked my opinion about local, state and international happenings. The person would nod sagely and then go about their business.

I would say to myself, *Who cares what I think! I'm just me and most of my so-called friends greet my ill-conceived pronouncements with howls of derision,* but I realised that I was considered to be an important member of the community and my opinions should be greeted with the respect they deserved!

Which also meant that I needed to watch what I said as anything I said, however frivolous or poorly expressed, would be taken seriously.

I can remember at least two occasions where this happened and I thought, each time, *What did I say and how did that happen as a result of it?*

The first was a really nice forty-two-year-old man called Tony, who worked very hard on the killing floor of the local abattoir. There, the newly slaughtered animals, suspended on an overhead chain moved across the floor and the meat-workers would dismember them. Sounds awful and it was. I would always feel quite queasy and off meat for a few days when I had to go out there. Thankfully, my memory didn't last too long as I am a confirmed meat eater.

Anyway, it was a high-pressure environment for the meat-workers and injuries such as lacerations, muscle strain and sprains, bad backs and dislocated digits were frequent occurrences.

Tony came to see me in the surgery one day with a dislocated little finger. Talking about the weather, by way of distraction, I gave it a good yank and put it back in place before Tony knew what had happened.

Tony then said, "This job is getting harder every year."

We then had a general discussion about the rigours of the meat-workers' job and I offered the thought that there were no sixty-five-year-old meat-workers as they all had to stop before retirement age due to injury.

Tony thanked me for my help and departed. Thinking about it later, I seemed to remember he had a somewhat far-away look in his eyes when he left me.

Blow me down but he came into the surgery a week later and said he had quit his job at the abattoir. He said, "I have you to thank for that, Doc!"

I thought, *What on earth have I done?*

Apparently, he used his considerable severance pay to purchase one of the local cafes. He not only made a good go of that but he also purchased a small delivery van and took a variety of delectable goodies out to the abattoir to provide lunches (at reasonable price, of course) for his ex-colleagues still working there.

He then branched out and did the same thing in the nearby regional centre – I had unleashed a café dynamo.

I saw him a few years ago and he hugged me fondly and said, "It was all down to you, Doc, thank you so much for your advice."

I thought about our apparently throwaway conversation all those years ago and how a seemingly innocuous discussion could have such far-reaching implications.

Just goes to show you how careful one has to be about mouthing off!

The second patient who took me literally, was a bit of a miserable sixty-ish woman who fitted well the description of a 'heart-sink patient'.

What is that? I hear you ask. Well, as you asked I will tell you!

They are the patients that every time they come to the surgery they make your heart sink!

They constantly complain about their lives, how ill they feel all the time, how nothing ever works out for them and generally what a dreadful existence they are forced to live on this earth. They are definitely a glass half-empty if not totally drained type of people.

One frequently does a lot of tests on them. Well, it's hard to think what to do for them and they think tests may help and you reassure yourself that you are not missing anything unpleasant. The tests invariably are normal. They have many real, and imagined, allergies and any treatment you suggest is frequently greeted with the statement that they have tried it before and it doesn't work or that they are allergic to it!

Basically, they seem to be people who are defeated by life. There is precious little medically wrong with them apart from varying degrees of depression. They just come into your room, dump all this shit on you and then leave. You are left feeling like you want to kill someone (usually them!) and are totally drained by the encounter.

A GP friend of mine used to keep a heavy medical book on his desk and when a 'heart-sink' person left, he would throw it at the door as it closed behind the departing patient!

I wonder if they, wreathed in misery largely of their own making, even noticed the thump.

Anyway, sorry about the rant, Gladys was one such patient. She was thin and wiry and clearly highly anxious, unconsciously wringing her hands during any consultation. She had a pinched and purse-lipped face and smoked incessantly, but thankfully not in the surgery. She had just about been exsanguinated by various tests over the years, which invariably were normal.

Once I suggested that I was obviously doing nothing for her and perhaps she should try another practitioner. After two weeks, she was back. Oh, dear!

She used to ask me about all kinds of things relating to her garden and the surgery staff reported that she would often be seen making large-scale renovations to either her house or garden based on some indifferent, casual advice from yours truly!

The final straw was when she came to see me complaining about her chest and the constant cough that plagued her.

I, somewhat casually, suggested a change in climate might help her respiratory problems.

With that, she sold her house and moved over a thousand kilometres to the north, into the tropics!

Again, what did I do, what did I say?

I haven't seen or heard from her or about her since then. No doubt she is now some other poor GP's 'heart-sink' patient. I hope my possibly ill-considered remark worked for her.

Ever since that time and those two cases in particular, I have been very careful about what I say to all patients; they might take me literally.

So, my general advice to anyone that cares to listen, is be careful of what you say!

Tension Pneumothorax
on a Gravel Rally

The southwest of our state has extensive areas of forest, which are used for timber logging and traversed by many dirt service roads.

These roads have a unique surface with a ball-bearing pea-sized type of gravel over a clay base. This makes the surface very slippery: Firstly, on the ball bearings themselves and secondly, on the clay base especially with a dash of rain thrown in.

Why am I telling you all this? Because it makes for fantastic car rallying. Overseas drivers say that it is the closest thing to driving on snow and ice that they have seen outside of Europe.

One of the events of the Australian Rally Championship (ARC) is held every year in the southwest and it is considered to be a considerable challenge by all the participants. They love it.

The story I want to relate, concerns that ARC event when it ran quite a few years ago.

I was the chief medical officer for the event, which sounds very grand but in reality, I was the only medical officer. There was an ambulance with two volunteer ambulance officers and that was the medical team. I was in my own 4x4 with a radio, a medical kit and moved around the stages, hoping to cover an area, which was quite geographically spread out.

These days things are much better organised with medical cars and crews on each stage but in those times, that was all we had.

On the first day of the rally, I was up at the furthest-away stage. I had stayed there for about half the field to go through and had just left to head to the next stage (some twenty kilometres away) when I got a radio call to say there had been an accident on the stage I had just departed.

I turned around and reached the start control (start line) a few minutes later.

The story was that a competitor had left the road some five kilometres into the stage and hit a tree.

With the stage commander leading in his car and I following in mine, we entered the stage and arrived at the accident site a few minutes later.

The vehicle had gone around a right-handed corner, which was badly cambered and tightened unexpectedly half way through it. Given the road surface of the gravel we talked of before, plus a light sprinkling of rain, the car had slid off the road and hit quite a substantial tree.

Interestingly one of the international drivers later said he had flagged that corner as a bad one and drove around it cautiously in second gear. Our less experienced driver went around the corner much faster, in fourth gear and unfortunately suffered the consequences.

When we arrived at the scene, the car was about 50 m off the left-hand side of the road, down a slight incline and wedged firmly against a large tree. In fact, the tree had intruded some 20 to 30 cms into the vehicle on the co-driver's (passenger) side.

Thankfully, rally cars have a well-constructed, exceedingly tough steel roll cage that forms literally a cage of steel around the crew. This had taken the brunt of the impact.

The driver was already out of the car but the co-driver was trapped inside. The tree was totally blocking his door (or what was left of it) and the roll cage had distorted, trapping his legs, fortunately without injuring them. His seat had moved slightly forward and he was sitting bolt upright, compressed by his safety harness with the top part of the roll cage broken with two jagged bits of steel piping sitting about 30 cms from him, aimed at his face!

A big, big impact, which had stopped just short of seriously, even fatally, injuring the trapped co-driver.

What to do?

Firstly, the car must be made safe so the battery isolator switch was flicked to turn off any power to the car. Thankfully, there was no fire so the built-in fire extinguishers did not have to be deployed.

The co-driver was talking normally but complaining of a bit of a sore chest.

I was able to get into the car via the passenger side rear door and do a quick assessment. Given the broken pieces of roll cage lurking about we elected the leave his helmet in place for protection while we got him out of the car.

Oh, yes! How do we get him out of the car then?

In those unenlightened days there was little, or more specifically no, Rescue Units or equipment close by to the rally. The nearest Rescue Unit (the Fire Brigade) was at a major regional town, some 100 kilometres away. That would take too long. He might well have had unsuspected injuries which could have caused a clinical deterioration in the two hours it would take for them to get to us – if he was trapped, and he was. All we could have done was, sit and watch!

There was however, the local Volunteer Bush Fire Brigade and their truck at the start of the stage.

Very carefully and gingerly, we attached a chain to the truck and the car, and oh so carefully, very slowly pulled the rally car off the tree. One has to be very cautious doing this as parts of the car, especially the roll cage can be under tension and spring back and behave unpredictably once that tension is released. A number of competitors have been injured over the years in that manner.

Luckily for the co-driver, all went well and the car was removed successfully from the tree's embrace.

The reduction of the tension on the roll cage enabled it to spring back slightly and release his legs. We were able to slide him onto a stretcher and get him out the driver's door. We then carried him back up to the roadway and placed him on the ambulance stretcher – the local ambulance having arrived a few minutes earlier.

I was then able to have a more thorough look at him.

As I was doing that, he started to complain of left-sided chest pain and increasing shortness of breath.

I wanted to listen to his breath sounds via my stethoscope but the background noise was incredible. Accident sites always have people quietly going about their jobs but also many more bustling around self-importantly, yelling unnecessary orders and discussing things loudly.

All I said was – "Shut the FUCK up!" – suddenly not a peep from anyone and I could listen to this guy's chest.

The result was not good – I could hear good breath sounds in the right lung but almost nothing on the left – he had a tension pneumothorax.

Let me explain.

Normally the lung is not attached or welded to the chest wall. Rather there is a thin film of liquid between the lung and the chest wall and since liquids are incompressible (remember your physics!) every time the chest wall moves, due to the surface tension of the liquid, so do the lungs, like when we expand our chest to breath in.

However, if air is introduced into the space the surface tension of the liquid between the lungs and the chest wall is lost and the lung falls away from the chest wall or collapses – medically this is known as a 'pneumothorax'. Most often this is when the lung is punctured.

There can be a further, rather nasty refinement of this, which is the 'Tension' pneumothorax. In this case there is a flap in the damaged area of the lung, which allows air into the new space between the lung surface and the chest wall when we breathe in but closes and traps the air when we breathe out. In this way, even a few breaths can build up volume and pressure in the space and eventually start compressing things like the remainder of the affected lung, the other lung and eventually the heart and the great vessels around it.

This can be fatal in as little as ten to fifteen minutes.

The thing to do is to put a drain into the space and release the air which is under increasing pressure. Usually that is done under sterile conditions in hospital and takes a while to set up and perform.

We, and more especially he, didn't have that sort of time.

The best emergency decompression is to use a large, long intravenous cannula (if you are interested usually a 14G x 5 cm). This is just put vertically into the chest, high up on the left side (to miss the heart and aorta etc.).

This I did and there was a very loud hiss of escaping air from the 'tension' – so loud in fact that someone about three metres away turned around and said, "What was that?"

That decompression is only a temporary but life-saving measure. A formal drain (called an ICC – Inter Costal Catheter) still needed to be inserted as the intravenous cannula can easily block off with movement etc.

He appeared to be otherwise okay, so my plan was to take him to the local hospital, some fifteen kilometres away, insert an ICC and then escort him to the regional hospital about an hour and a half away.

Seemed like a plan.

However, once we were back in phone reception (there was none at the accident site although we did have radios), we learned that there had been a tragedy at the local hospital and the single room in their emergency department was occupied by a fourteen-year-old Down's syndrome girl who had just died from severe asthma. How ghastly!

The staff very kindly agreed to move this poor girl's body into a private room in the hospital so the family could spend their last, quiet moments with her.

We felt dreadful and very subdued when we arrived. The ICC was inserted and off we set for the regional hospital, some 90 minutes away.

When we arrived there, I was relieved to see an old colleague of mine and he arranged for a number of investigations including a chest X-ray to ensure the ICC was in the correct place. Thankfully it was but there was one further twist in the tale to play out.

My colleague and I both looked at the chest X-ray and both of us thought that the mediastinum (the bit in the middle of the CXR which is usually white compared to the darker lungs and this is the bit that contains the heart and the great vessels) looked to be wider than normal. Was something going on in this very vital and dangerous area?

A CT scan confirmed that there was a tear in the aorta, the main supply vessel from the heart to the body. Thankfully it was a small partial tear. If completely torn, the person would die almost immediately!

Later that day, he was flown to the capital city by the Royal Flying Doctor Service and had the aorta repaired in an operation lasting some five hours.

What a lucky guy!

Unfortunately, his new bride was not similarly impressed as she had been very nervous about the whole rally exercise and had implored him not to take part.

Needless to say, he has not been rallying since.

Annabelle

Annabelle came to town with her husband and three children approximately thirty weeks into her fourth pregnancy. They lived out of town a little, in a rented asbestos and tile house, set back from the road with hundred metres of gravel driveway linking them.

They had moved down from the north of the state where her husband, Michael, had been working. He came to our town to do a similar job.

At that time, the northern town where they had come from had been terrorised by a serial rapist, which had made the family nervous as Michael often worked long hours. That problem had, in part, precipitated the family's move. The other thing was that Michael had bought a .22 rifle for protection.

Annabelle herself was a quiet, unprepossessing, woman in her early thirties. Physically she was slim with somewhat rounded shoulders and poor posture. She had lank, straight brown hair and sleepy eyes. One might almost say 'bedroom eyes' – you know that half-lidded look – but in her case it just made you feel tired. When I first met her, she had that quiet air of defeat about her that you see sometimes, as if life was just a little too much for her.

She came to see me at the surgery to continue her antenatal care and deliver the baby at the hospital. She made no great impression on me, one way or the other. I can't recall any major problems during the seven or eight visits to the surgery or with the subsequent rather straightforward delivery.

The problems started about two to three days post-delivery when both mother and child were doing well.

I was away for a week and both my partners kept an eye on her whilst she was in the hospital. In those days we had the luxury of being able to keep mothers in hospital longer than now, a particular bonus if there were several children at home.

Annabelle had become concerned that the baby had a number of pimples on her face. I might say that this is not unusual in the newborn, as the skin moves from producing the cold cream like vernix to the clear waxy sebum of normal skin. The pores often get a bit clogged.

Anyway, one of the doctors noticed her perturbation and wrote a script for a topical cream, which besides containing a number of topical antibiotics, also contains a small amount of corticosteroid.

The next day the doctor, on his rounds, noticed that Annabelle was dabbing the spots with cream every few seconds. She would peer anxiously at the baby's cheek, shake her head, reach for the cream and put a small dab on the offending area. Time after time!

My colleague remonstrated with her and told her that prolonged use of topical steroid would eventually cause skin atrophy and breakdown. Well, that stopped her in her tracks. Instead she then became fixated on the idea that the child had skin atrophy.

Each morning on the ward round, she would waylay us all and hold the baby's blemish-less face for our perusal saying, "Look, look, can't you see her skin is atrophied." She would be briefly mollified by the reassurances from us but within a few minutes would again be accosting staff displaying the baby's pristine face for their inspection. It drove the busy midwives nuts and they were pleased to see her go home a few days later.

She then used to come into the surgery on an almost daily basis, bringing the baby so I could examine the ravages wrought by steroid on her face. Again, she appeared to accept reassurance that all was well but within a few moments would say, "Look at her face. Look at her face. Am I the only one that can see it?" Believe me, this is the last thing you need on a busy Monday morning with a full booking list and the waiting room filling up. Sometimes it would take me up to half an hour to ease her out of the consulting room.

I also noticed that her expression was more deadpan than usual, what is known in the trade as a 'flat affect'. The only time she was at all animated was when she was expostulating on the evils of that bloody steroid cream. About now I was wishing that the muck had never been invented in the first place.

I became increasingly concerned with her affect and general demeanour. I was very afraid she had a bad case of postnatal depression. Michael was similarly concerned. He reported that Annabelle was functioning okay at home and looking after the kids including the newborn but would spend a lot of the time staring at the wall and get up at odd times during the night to check on the baby's skin.

When I spoke to her about this possibility, she seemed to have no insight, maintaining that all was well and that everything would resolve once the atrophy was under control. I arranged for her and Michael to see the regional psychiatrist in the regional centre.

This visit was not a success and the expert opinion was all was well. Her bizarre behaviour continued. We then arranged for her to go to a metropolitan hospital and see the psychiatrists there. At least they admitted her. She stayed there for a couple of weeks and had some anti-depressive medications before being discharged home 'cured'.

Some cure. Michael told me that Annabelle went out to her parents' place in the city on day leave from the ward and when he went to visit, he found her on the floor of the darkened dining room, curled in a foetal position, rocking back and forth, moaning. Her mother told him that nothing was wrong. Perhaps that's where Annabelle got it.

Within a few days, she was back to 'normal' bizarre behaviour. The metropolitan 'psychs' were then contacted and basically weren't interested.

Then there followed a sad progression through a number of private psychiatrists, all of whom told us that nothing was wrong. The last one even told Michael that he was the one with a mental problem and needed help. If the poor bugger didn't before, he had to be coming close by now. Michael also told me that Annabelle had had a half-hearted attempt to throw herself in front of a car in a shopping centre car park.

The scene now shifts forward by about a week from when Michael got the revelation on high that he was nuts too. It was a Saturday and I was in the small Emergency Department at our hospital sewing up someone's hand, who had been a bit boisterous with the bread knife. The phone rings...

Have I told you how the ambulance system worked in the bush where the 'ambos' are all volunteers?

In the city and major centres, you dial 000 and get put through to central dispatcher and an ambulance is sent to you, prioritised on your perceived need. Not so in the bush at that time. Then you rang the hospital, who then rang the volunteer ambos at home, who then got into their uniforms, drove to the depot, picked up the ambulance and then drove to where they were needed. This can take up to 15 to 20 minutes.

Anyway, where was I? Oh yes, the phone rings...

It is Michael. He is crying and barely coherent. He wants an ambulance. Annabelle has just shot herself with that .22 rifle they had bought for 'protection'.

The bread knife twit is forgotten. Everything is dropped and I race outside to my car, knowing that the ambulance will be at least 10 minutes behind me. Spectacular F1-type take-off with my mind just having gone blank. A couple of minutes later I turn into their semi-rural street.

As I turn into the hundred-metre drive leading to the house, the eldest son (about twelve years old) comes racing down the drive toward me screaming with his hands waving in the air. I slow down expecting some sort of conference with him. He just goes straight past me, yelling incoherently. *Oh, shit!* I thought.

I get to the house and go inside. Michael is sobbing quietly and clutching his young daughter and wordlessly points into the passage. And, there is Annabelle.

She is lying in the passage on her back, looking quite peaceful. Her hands are by her side and she is not moving. Her eyes are closed and there is a bullet hole in the centre of her forehead. The rifle is by her side.

Her hair is fanned out a little bit like the sun's rays or the bayonet emblem of the badge of the Australian Army. A perfect fan, held in place by blood. Medusa-like.

By this stage, I'm not feeling that good myself and half-collapse, half-kneel by her side. Looking at her, lying peacefully with her eyes closed, I lean forward so I'm about a foot from her face and call her name, "Annabelle, Annabelle, what have you done?"

Suddenly her eyes open wide, with me about a foot away. I almost crapped myself. I thought she was dead for sure. Now I do collapse and sit down next to her.

The next ten minutes seem to take forever. She gazes at me fixedly. We are able to have some communication of sorts. She blinks once for yes and twice for no.

"Are you in pain?" Two blinks.

"Do you have a headache?" (What a stupid bloody question!) One blink.

I can't really recall what other questions I asked but they were probably as silly as the previous ones.

At last the ambulance arrives and we load her onto the stretcher for the trip to the hospital. The carpet underneath where her head had lain will never be the same.

I assess her more fully at the hospital. She is conscious and looking after her airway well. She still blinks at us in reply to queries. My senior partner suggests that perhaps the bullet hasn't penetrated her skull. Fat chance.

Her skull X-ray looks like a melon that has been hit with an axe. The left side is split and leaning toward the left. On the lateral (sideways view) the bullet (hollow nose variety) is spread from the front to the back.

She will need to go to the city to see the neurosurgeons. I speak to them, load her into the ambulance for the two-hour trip and off we go. The trip up is uneventful; Annabelle is surprisingly composed. Perhaps she has given herself a *Frontal Leucotomy*, the old operation used to calm down aggressive schizophrenics.

The neurosurgeons remove most of the bullet and the accompanying blood clot and thus started her long period of convalescence. She came back to town about six weeks later and continued to have intensive physiotherapy at the really good practice down the road.

If anything, Annabelle was even quieter than before. She doggedly went about looking after the kids, not without some difficulty. Medically, she appeared okay with the only residual deficit being an inability to lift her right foot up, known as a 'foot drop'.

Michael never felt the same about Annabelle once she came home. He was very short with her inability to do the things that she had done previously. When he brought her to the practice, he appeared to be constantly angry with her and took opportunities to belittle her. I heard on the grapevine that on one occasion the family locked her out of the house and she forlornly limped from window to window and door to door, tapping pathetically for admission.

I remember well, the day she came to see me about six months after the shooting. Annabelle was the best I had ever seen her. She was positively animated. She told me that she at last realised what she had done to herself and to the family, and she could feel that from now on she was going to get better. I was delighted and tried to be as encouraging as I could be.

She said that she only had one thing that was worrying her. Each time she put both hands in water, as when doing the washing up, the left one felt normal but the right one tingled a lot. Like pins and needles.

I spoke to the consultant neurosurgeon who said that altered sensation was not unusual in cases like hers but to be on the safe side, we should do a CT scan of her brain. Sounded like a good idea.

The scan results came back a day later. They showed that there were three, two-to-three centimetre 'coin lesions' in Annabelle's brain. The consensus was that they were secondary cancers.

Where had they come from? They certainly weren't there when she had extensive investigation by the neurosurgeons, including a number of CTs, some six months previously.

Apparently, she had had a 'mole' removed in the north when they were up there some years ago. It was a superficial melanoma, completely excised. No follow-up was done. She was never told about the potential seriousness of the lesion.

Biopsy confirmed the brain lesions were indeed secondary melanomas.

Annabelle died six months later.

Had a microscopic secondary cancer affected her behaviour enough to precipitate that dreadful sequence of events? I don't know, and I suppose that we never will know.

What do you think?

The Hapless Dr Lee

In the early days of this century, a nearby country hosted the Formula 1 Grand Prix for a few years.

A circuit was built, at vast expense, near a town in the south of the country about five hours by road from the capital.

The Australian motor sport governing body, CAMS (Confederation of Australian Motor Sport) was contracted to provide technical and training support for the local team running the event. This is not as silly as it may sound, if a country has not run an F1 event before (Or an Olympics for that matter). They are usually not across the stringent requirements demanded by the governing body (In this case, the Federation Internationale d'Automobile – FIA) before the event is allowed to happen. Australia had done it before and therefore, we went to help.

I was fortunate to be involved on the medical side of things and indeed I was the Chief Medical Officer (CMO) for most of the four years that the event ran.

During the year before the first event, I visited the country several times to talk to the local medical team and do some preparatory training. I was struck by the language barrier that existed. While I freely admit, I spoke not a word of the language (I eventually learnt 'Thank you'!), I only recall about three locals who spoke fluent English and were able to communicate easily with me.

However, besides a lack of English, no one understood the Australian idiom, so I had to be very careful not to descend into my usual slang!

The locals I met were universally nice. They were very keen to make the event successful and went out of their way to be helpful. Never wanting to offend, any question would invariably be met with 'Yes' or 'Maybe', never a 'No'. I learnt that the 'Yes' and 'Maybe' sometimes did indeed mean 'No', but they were just too polite to say it. Frustrating at times, but I got used to it.

I took quite a team of medicos from Australia for the first actual event.

As part of the medical set-up, there were a number of Medical Intervention Vehicles (MIVs) placed at strategic points around the circuit. These have a medical staff of two, (usually a doctor plus another doctor or paramedic) a driver and good emergency medical equipment. They were able to rapidly respond, under the direction of Race Control, to any incident. Each of the MIVs for the first event had an Australian doctor to help and train the other MIV crew.

In addition, there were two Extrication Teams (again mixed Australian and locals), which had all the necessary equipment such as cutters and spreaders to be able to extricate a driver from their wrecked vehicle if necessary.

Added to that, the FIA requires a well set-up, staffed and equipped medical centre to be at the circuit. This enabled the stabilisation of any casualties before their evacuation to the major trauma centre, some eighty kilometres away.

There were also two dedicated helicopters on site at the medical centre to enable any evacuation to be effected with minimal delay.

So that was the set-up. All set and raring to go!

The FIA have a number of delegates that it sends to each of its different championship events, including F1. There are technical delegates, who ensure that all the F1 cars comply with the technical regulations; there is the Race Control team which includes the Race Director who is in overall charge of the event; plus his extensive communications team; and the FIA F1 Medical Delegate.

The FIA Medical Delegate, as the name suggests, ensures that all the regulations pertaining to the medical side of the event, not only at the track but also at the receiving hospitals, are in accordance with 'best practice' and the FIA regulations.

He also travels in the FIA Medical Car, which follows or 'chases' the first lap of the F1 race itself and thereafter is stationed at pit-lane exit to respond to any significant incident at the behest of the Race Director. Beside the FIA Medical Delegate, there is always a doctor from the country that the event is being held in the medical car, as the delegate is not necessarily registered to practice medicine in each of the countries that the F1 series go to.

Before the event begins in earnest, there is always a Medical Exercise where a medical scenario is set up and one of the MIVs (selected at random, though usually warned before!) responds to.

Usually a mock-up of a FI car cockpit (called 'the tub') is placed somewhere around the track and a script read to the attending members of the MIV crew, upon arrival at the 'accident' scene. They are then required to take the appropriate action to stabilise and treat the driver.

At that time, there was quite an advanced programmable mannequin which was placed in the tub cockpit and that could be made to do various things and display different medical conditions, some of them not very nice at all!

On this occasion, the tub and mannequin were placed at Turn 4, some three kilometres from the pit lane exit. As there was an Australian doctor in each of the MIVs, it was decided to deploy the FIA Medical Car from pit-lane exit for the exercise.

Enter Dr Lee, who was the local doctor assigned to the FIA Medical Car.

All the other MIV and Extrication crew were at Turn 4 to watch the fun and learn, fervently thanking their lucky stars that they were not the one having to do the scenario. The Extrication team at Turn 4 remained in their vehicles in case they were needed for the exercise. The tub was set up and the mannequin programmed.

On this occasion, the mannequin was programmed to have a breathing rate of three per minute (very, very slow) and a single dilated pupil, indicating an intra-cranial bleed, rapidly expanding, and pressing on vital structures in the brain.

What this 'patient' needs is immediate removal from the car, assistance with breathing (The way he is going, he will stop breathing by himself soon.) and then rapid transport to the medical centre with ongoing evacuation to a neurosurgical facility. At times like this, other injuries such as spinal injuries are secondary considerations as the patient will shortly expire because of not breathing, rather than because there is a chance their neck is broken. So, get them out of the car as quickly as possible.

So off we go and the exercise starts.

The medical communicator makes a call to the FIA Medical Car and it is 'scrambled' from pit-lane exit to the scene. We can hear its sirens as it approaches. Travelling at a fair old lick, it screeches to an impressive halt near the tub and the crew leap out, including Dr Lee. The driver is kindly carrying the medical bag.

Game on!

Dr Lee runs up to the tub but stops a couple of metres away. With a look of intense concentration, he circles the tub a number of times. At no stage does he approach the 'patient' closer than one to two metres. What is going on?

The FIA Medical Delegate gently asks him what he is going to do next. His response is another couple of circuits of the tub!

About now, I'm thinking, *Well, this is going well – not!*

Urgently but surreptiously, I signal to the nearby Extrication team to please, please come and help. They respond manfully (…and woman-fully as there are a couple of women in the team.) and in no time, do an emergency extrication of the 'patient' and lay 'him' on the ground.

The medical delegate then asks Dr Lee what he would like to do now. He is still about one metre away from the 'patient'.

There is a light-bulb moment.

"Oxygen!" he cries.

He is then handed an oxygen cylinder complete with attached giving set. The 'patient's' respiratory rate has not increased above three per minute (You or I normally breath at 12 to 15 breaths a minute).

He gets the oxygen mask onto the mannequin and then attaches the other end to the locking key that affixes the giving set to the cylinder, rather than the oxygen delivery nipple! No oxygen for this patient! What 'he' needs is his ventilation (breathing) to be assisted by a bag and mask.

Satisfied, Dr Lee stands back and is asked what he would like to do now.

"Go to the medical centre!"

The awaiting ambulance crew put the mannequin onto their stretcher and load 'him' into the back of the ambulance, all the time with Dr Lee standing by, without offering assistance and still not getting within one metre of the 'patient'.

"Are you going to go with him to the medical centre?" asks the medical delegate.

"Yes!" replies Dr Lee and races around to sit in the front of the ambulance! It is gently pointed out to him that, since he has a very unwell 'patient', he might like to ride in the back of the ambulance with 'him' and render assistance for the short journey to the medical centre.

Off they go. Lights and sirens – the full spec!

We load the tub into the back of a second ambulance and make our way back to the medical centre. This takes about ten minutes and when we arrive, the first ambulance with Dr Lee and the 'patient' under full 'bells and whistles', is nowhere to be seen.

Where are they?

Unfortunately, they have taken a wrong turn and now are circling around the 'in-field', vainly looking for access to the medical centre which is in another area entirely.

Finally, after another ten minutes they arrive, lights and sirens flashing and wailing impressively. They sweep into the ambulance bay, throw open the back doors and wrench the stretcher out.

The now definitely moribund 'patient' is thrown onto the ground as the stretcher spectacularly collapses!

"I think we'll stop it there," says the FIA medical delegate.

So that was it. I certainly have been to better F1 medical exercises but I struggle to remember one that was worse.

Now I may have been unkind to Dr Lee in the telling of this story.

He actually was a very well-respected surgeon (besides being a very nice guy) but not at all used to front line trauma response. The good thing about being a surgeon is that the patients are usually all nicely packaged and resuscitated by the time they reach the operating theatre.

Unfortunately for the first year, most of the emergency physicians were away on a course and therefore unavailable to us. He had very kindly stepped into unfamiliar territory to help.

Dr Lee was a little out of his depth but gave it a shot. In the later years, he became the 'quarter-master' for the medical team. Ask him for anything that you wanted, often by showing a photo of the equipment needed, and it would be there the next day. He was brilliant in that role.

So, there you have it. Not all of us can 'be all things, to all men' but eventually we can all find a niche where we can excel.

Resuscitation at the Surgery

It was the start of what appeared to be a normal day at our main surgery in our town. The three GPs (myself being one) were getting down to business – the waiting room slowly filling, our lateness just starting to show and our office manager beginning to think about ringing patients with later appointments to have a cup of coffee down town and delay their arrival.

Tim, one of my partners, ushered in this sixty-three-year-old man called Bert from out of town, who informed him he had been having intermittent chest and jaw pain overnight. Every time this happened he got a bit shaky and breathless but his wife had not been sleeping well lately so he did not want to wake her up and worry her unnecessarily.

He came in to see Tim somewhat apologetic and diffident. Thankfully he had no chest pain at that time so Tim popped him into our treatment room for the practice staff to do an ECG.

I was half way through a patient consultation, I can't for the life of me remember about what, when there was a pounding at my door. The office manager flew in unannounced to say that the ECG man Bert had just had a cardiac arrest in the treatment room.

When I arrived, Tim was doing cardiac compressions and we agreed I would look after the airway.

Now. The airway and, of course, breathing.

When we are awake, we happily breathe in and out, eat and drink, swallow saliva etc. without (mostly) either air of food/drink/saliva 'going down the wrong way'. Sometimes we do get it wrong and a spectacular episode of coughing and spluttering ensues. A little flap of gristle, the epiglottis, closes over our trachea (the entrance to the airway and lungs) to prevent food, drink etc. going into the lungs and directs it into the oesophagus or gullet sitting immediately behind the trachea. Neat, eh?

If we are unconscious, say like what happens when you have a cardiac arrest (Well, you are not particularly well, are you?), your normal airway protection mechanisms are not working and you can inhale material (especially vomit) into your lungs.

As the patient is unconscious, the muscle tone around the upper airway (the pharynx, larynx and tongue) is lost and they tend to become floppy and obstruct the airway. Incidentally, that floppiness, often due to obesity or semi-consciousness induced by drugs or alcohol, is a significant cause of sleep apnoea.

In a two-pronged attack, firstly the reduced muscle tone runs the risk of obstructing the upper airway but secondly inhaling stuff into the lungs, especially the stomach contents, is generally considered to be a *bad* thing. Not only does the liquid vomit fill a part of the lung and interfere with gas exchange but solid vomit, such as chunks – sorry to be gross – can block a major airway and effectively shut down a segment of lung. Also, the acid can cause a very nasty inflammation/infection in the part of the lung it affects.

The first part of getting air into the patient is, making sure the upper airway is open and not obstructed by the tongue, food or even loose dentures. There are a couple of manoeuvres, such as the chin lift and jaw thrust that facilitate this. Only when upper airway patency is achieved can thought be given to breathing for the patient.

The simplest form of this is Expired Air Resuscitation (EAR) or Mouth to Mouth. I have heard people say, "Well, that's not much use as you have used all the oxygen in your last breath; so, then giving it to someone else won't do any good." Not so. Air has an oxygen content of 21% but when you breathe out (as in mouth to mouth), the oxygen content in the air going into the patient is still 16%.

A more sophisticated form of assisted breathing is to use a bag and mask (with or without oxygen attached). This is basically a semi-rigid bag reservoir of about one-litre capacity connected to a mask that fits snuggly over the patient's mouth and nose. The bag is squeezed and, provided the upper airway is open, air (twenty-one per cent oxygen) enters the lungs. A valve on the mask ensures that the expired air from the patient does not re-enter the bag. Oxygen tubing can be attached which therefore, increases the percentage of oxygen in each breath given to the patient this way.

Both these methods work well if done properly. The bag and mask have obvious advantages in that there is less direct intimate contact with the patient – important in this age of hepatitis and HIV. However, in a resuscitation, the survival of another human being is in the balance so such considerations, quite rightly, should be secondary to the main task. Anyway, in our society as it was then, the chance of catching anything nasty was almost non-existent.

The rub is that if the airway is not opened sufficiently, the air entering the person may be directed to the stomach and inflate that. I have been to a number of resuscitations over the years were this has happened and the abdomen visibly distends followed almost inevitably by loud burping and regurgitation of stomach contents with the all the potential problems we discussed before.

The next step up in the airways stakes is to intubate the patient, This, involves using an instrument called a laryngoscope which is inserted into the (unconscious) patient's mouth, slides over the tongue to the base of the epiglottis (the gristle flap we mentioned earlier) and gives direct vision of the vocal cords and the trachea. Under direct vision a tube, a bit like and the size of a section of garden hose, is introduced into the trachea. There is an inflatable cuff which is blown up which therefore stops any material (vomit, blood etc.) getting into the lungs and causing mischief.

This is a huge advantage as the patient's airway is now safe. We have gone from an essentially unprotected airway, vulnerable to inhaling anything about the place, to an airway that now ends in a tube which is protected and outside the mouth to which can be attached any sort of mechanical breathing device you want from the bag and mask to a full ventilator.

These days, there are other airway devices and intubation methods available such as video guided laryngoscopes and laryngeal masks but at that time in the 1980s, these were not available.

Anyway, sorry about the lengthy and perhaps pedantic explanation – let's get back to Bert.

Bert had neither a spontaneously beating heart or any spontaneous breathing.

Tim was doing a good job with the chest compressions, basically squashing the heart between a rock and a hard place that is between the bony vertebral column (backbone) and the flat bony plate of the sternum (breastbone). Surprisingly, good CPR can achieve approximately 10% to 40% of the output of the normal heart – not enough for long-term purposes but certainly enough to keep the brain alive while other measures are put in place.

As I said, Bert was not breathing and – not only that – had vomited slightly and had a small amount of greenish vomit around his lips. Charming!

I wiped that away, got our ancient bag and mask out, plus a guedel airway which is put into the mouth and stops the tongue from flopping back and obstructing the airway. Unfortunately, the bag was so old that the rubber was perished and it gave up the ghost after a couple of puffs. Great!

I then made the decision to intubate Bert, having the tube and the laryngoscope easy to hand. I got a good view down the trachea with the laryngoscope and passed the tube easily into the airway.

Unfortunately, there was still quite a bit of vomit in the upper airway. We usually use a sucker to remove that so let's get it. Oh, that's right! We don't have any suction set up at the surgery.

What to do? Well, all I could do was to suck it out myself and spit it onto the floor! Sounds incredibly gross but funnily enough I didn't even think of that at the time (I do now however, and shudder occasionally!)

By that time, Bill, our third partner had arrived and started putting in an intravenous line. (For drugs etc.)

I looked up at him, he now recalls, with a ring of vomit around my mouth and asked if he would like to take over the airway. As we were all pretty hyped up at this stage, his shout of laughter was very loud and undoubtedly heard all over the surgery! Tim was not amused!

We had got things relatively stable by now with good CPR in progress and Bert pinking up a bit.

We sent to the local hospital (about five minutes away) for an oxygen cylinder (which also has suction – too late!) and the defibrillator. We had neither of these bits of equipment at the surgery. Oh, and I nearly forgot, a slightly newer ventilating bag.

Once the orderly arrived from the hospital we were able to attach the new bag with oxygen and use that to give Bert breaths. Up until then he had been getting by with me blowing down the tube.

We gave Bert some IV adrenaline to stimulate the heart and the defibrillator indicated that he had ventricular fibrillation (That is a heart rhythm instead of the thousands of heart muscle fibres beating synchronously together. They just do their own thing and beat independently which means there is no coordinated contraction of heart muscle and therefore, no cardiac output at all).

Fortunately, this is what is called a shockable rhythm – if you shock the heart muscle the individual fibres stop being silly and if you are lucky, they commence beating together and doing their normal job.

We shocked Bert once. Nothing. Back to CPR. Another shock. Again nothing, so back to CPR. More adrenaline. More shocks.

We shocked Bert about nine times. The battery on the defibrillator was showing 'low' and we were about to give up. We had been resuscitating Bert for nearly 45 minutes and were nearing the end.

One last shock and for some unknown, unimagined, wonderful reason, Bert's heart just restarted and pumped away as if nothing had happened. Bloody thing!

Bert was now stable – yes, we were breathing for him but his heart had spontaneous output and he was perfusing all his vital organs, most importantly the brain, all by himself.

We escorted Bert to the major teaching hospital in the capital city some two hours away by ambulance where he had heart surgery for coronary bypass grafts (No stents in those days!).

About six weeks later, Bert and his wife came to our surgery with gifts for everyone and admonished us for breaking his ribs.

A charge we were delighted to be able to plead guilty to!

Primum Non Nocere
(FIRST, DO NO HARM)

Longer ago than I care to remember, I was a fourth-year medical student attached to a surgical team at one of the major tertiary hospitals in our capital city.

In that term, we would usually have lectures or something like that for an hour or so during the day and the rest of the time we would be in the operating theatres (mainly getting in the way) and on the surgical wards and on occasions when the team was 'on take', go down to the Emergency Department (ED) and 'clerk' (do a medical history and examination) the patients who were to be admitted under our team that day.

It was on such a 'take' day that we met Edward Bear.

Edward was a somewhat forgettable, pleasant enough, inoffensive sixty-one-year-old government clerk. Pleasingly he seemed somewhat in awe of the medical profession and even by extension medical students such as us.

The problem that he presented with to ED was one of constipation. Like many before him, he had started with a period of diarrhoea for which he took tablets to bind himself up.

In this aim, he had spectacularly succeeded and indeed had not had a bowel motion for the preceding ten days! Anyone who has ever been constipated will appreciate the dreadful, agonising abdominal cramps that accompany this condition. Due to the back up of poo, in effect the poor patient has a functional bowel obstruction.

Anyway this had happened to poor Edward and he was in agony.

The usual treatment is to try and clear the blockage from below with such charming devices as enemas (Inserted in the rectum, in the old days soap and water, but in this more enlightened age various active chemicals.) and the intriguingly named manual removal – neither of these are for the faint hearted or those with delicate tummies (staff that is!).

So Edward was given and enema, which did nothing; all he did was to return the enema with no other 'result'. For some reason that escapes me, any success from this treatment is always known as 'the result'!

Anyway, no result from the enema. So he was given another one, perhaps a slightly fiercer version.

Again no result, so a manual removal was attempted. As the name suggests this means the staff members' hands/fingers are inserted into the patient's rectum via the anus and handfuls of poo are pulled out, hopefully clearing the blockage. Bloody painful for the patient and very queasy making for the poor staff member concerned. It always makes me vomit.

The staff member doing the manual removal, set out with a will and displayed such enthusiasm that he/she managed to perforate the rectum. In other words, put a hole in the wall of the rectum allowing communication between the bowel and the abdominal (peritoneal) cavity.

This is generally considered to be a 'bad' thing and can lead to peritonitis and even death from overwhelming sepsis if not detected.

In Edward's case, this potential disaster was compounded by the fact that he was given a third enema which again did nothing apart from filling his abdominal cavity with a delightful combination of poo and soapy water!

To say – this greatly increased Edward's discomfiture – is a gross understatement. Besides that, it was now a medical/surgical emergency that required rapid intervention if overwhelming peritonitis and sepsis were to be prevented.

So off we all went to the operating theatre.

The consultant surgeon was not in attendance (he was away at a conference – entirely appropriate.). So his senior registrar, another registrar and the resident (the next three in descending order in the surgical team hierarchy) were gowned and gloved and around the operating table doing the operation, two anaesthetists were in attendance, three scrub nurses and three medical students including myself against the back wall trying to be inconspicuous – quite a lot of people for one small operating theatre!

All was in readiness for us to help poor old Edward. Before going under the anaesthetic, he expressed his thanks for all the things the staff had done and were going to do for him.

The operation required a large incision basically from the bottom of the sternum (breastbone) to the pubic bone to allow maximal exposure to find and close the hole in the rectum but also, importantly, to wash out all the poo and soap mixture from the abdominal cavity.

This was expeditiously done but unfortunately during the retraction of the left-hand side of the incision (to allow greater visualisation of the abdomen), the retractor damaged the spleen, which started to bleed profusely. The splenic artery was therefore clamped and the entire spleen removed (once 'pranged', the spleen, which essentially a large friable bag of blood, cannot be stitched up like many other organs).

So, post-operatively Edward was left with a large wound, which had a lot of tension type sutures to hold it together; the absence of a previously happily functioning spleen (People can get by without a spleen but it makes them more prone to certain types of infection.) and on heroic doses of intra-venous antibiotics.

The antibiotics were very necessary to counter the possibility of any infection arising from Edward's misfortunes to date.

Anyway, (there is that word again!) – post-operatively – Edward seemed to be doing well and we, as medical students, would visit him every day or so to check on his progress. He again often expressed his thanks for the care and expertise that was being lavished upon him.

A few days after the operation, it was noted that Edward's albumin (a protein found in the blood) was low and his hearing seemed to have deteriorated somewhat.

One of the antibiotics, Gentamycin, a powerful and effective drug is also known to have unfortunate side effects such as attacking the kidneys (Initiating kidney failure and causing them to lose albumin from the blood into the urine – hence the low level.) and attacking the hair cells in the inner ear and precipitating irreversible damage to them and deafness.

This had happened to Edward whose kidneys were now decidedly second-hand as was his hearing.

He became a little dizzy and unwell, though still grateful, and got out of bed one day, fell and managed to open up his entire wound. This necessitated a return to the operating theatre to stitch him up again. Unfortunately, he was not as good anaesthetic risk as his previous visit to the theatre some three weeks previously.

Edward came through the second operation relatively well and returned to our surgical ward for post-operative care but he started to get a fever despite his intravenous antibiotic administration (Gentamycin had been ceased some time previously).

Edward died after just over four weeks in our surgical ward from kidney failure and sepsis, still pathetically grateful for everything the medical profession had done for him.

I have thought of Edward, on and off, all my professional career. He serves as a constant reminder to me that, however well-intentioned we are, we sometimes get things wrong and the warning is that we must never compound one error on top of another and that the price of security for ourselves, and our patients, is constant vigilance.

Vale Edward Bear and thank you! I have never forgotten what you taught me. Perhaps that is a fitting memorial.

The Premature Twins

Dom and Anna lived on a little farm on the banks of the river some way out of town. They had some citrus and cows. A smallholding. They weren't well off but made a go of things. As yet they had not had any kids.

Anna was quite a pretty girl but very shy and somewhat retiring. Somewhere in her genetic make-up was a gene that gave her very prominent, googly eyes. Varying doctors had just about bled her dry, testing for overactive thyroid but invariably the results came back as normal.

After they had been married for a year or so, Anna came to me thinking that she was pregnant. I gained the impression that she was quite embarrassed by that possibility and that talking about such matters as sex and procreation was, for her, a bit beyond the bounds of politeness.

So, she came in to see me for her first antenatal visit somewhat diffidently and we went through the usual manner of talking about what would happen during the pregnancy, organising some screening tests and a vague allusion (which made her look even more uncomfortable) to the then distant confinement and delivery.

It was my usual practice to arrange a foetal ultrasound at about eleven weeks. As the ultrasound was in the nearest regional centre, an hour away, I used to only do one ultrasound during the pregnancy unless there was a good clinical reason to do another. Generally, the earlier the ultrasound, the better the dating and the later the ultrasound the better the look at the foetal anatomy. So, eleven weeks was a good compromise. This gave the best combination of accurate dating and a bit of a look at foetal anatomy.

Anyway, Anna went off to have her eleven-week ultrasound and shock, horror, joy or rapture (take your pick)! She was having twins!

Now we were lucky in the town to be only about an hour away from a major regional centre, which had the services of a specialist obstetrician. No GP in his right mind would voluntarily deliver a twin pregnancy, especially in a 'primip' (primipara, someone having their first baby), when there is an obstetrician within 'Cooee'.

What usually happens is that we do shared care. I see the pregnant mum for most of her antenatal visits with occasional early visits to the obstetrician. As the fateful date approaches, more frequently, during the last few weeks, she will see only the obstetrician. Usually works well.

Anna, once she found out that she was having twins, was even more nervous and twitchy about the whole process. She often would rush into the surgery with real or imagined problems, which thankfully were either the normal vagaries of pregnancy (multiplied because of the twins) or nothing at all, which just needed a good dose of reassurance. Pregnant mums, especially first timers, are always a bit twitchy so I never minded checking them out and reassuring them. I should add, I also like to reassure myself. You can never be too careful and just sometimes something is going on which, if you pick it up early, can be fixed without causing any major hassles.

The scene now shifts to the Monday morning surgery, always a busy time. I have a medical student with me, so I'm travelling a little slower than normal. I am getting behind. The staff is already ringing up people to tell them to come later than their appointment time as we are running late. It is only 10.30 a.m. Great!

Then, in comes an especially nervous looking Anna. Just what I need!

I escort her into my consulting room and introduce her to the medical student, having first asked her privately if it is okay that he stays in the room for the consultation.

She is looking even more uncomfortable than normal. Perhaps it is the presence of the student, so I ask him to go and check on some results and he with remarkable good grace for one so young, excuses himself and leaves. He'll go far, I think to myself.

Anna relaxes slightly and then tells me that she is having contractions. Yeah, right, I think to myself so to humour her. I get her up on the consulting bed and put my hand on her tummy.

Bloody hell! She is having contractions! What are we going to do now?

The first thing to do is an internal examination to feel if the cervix (the neck or opening of the uterus or womb) is dilated. When a baby (or in this case babies) is delivered the first thing that happens is that the cervix dilates, so it/they can get out of the womb and be delivered. Normally the cervix is closed and won't admit an examining finger but just before delivery it is dilated up to about ten centimetres. Most of a confinement is spent, increasingly painfully I might add, waiting for the cervix to dilate. Only then can one embark on the even more painful process of pushing the 'Bloody thing out!'

Anyway, I needed to examine Anna to see if her cervix had dilated at all.

Sounds fairly straightforward but Anna had a problem called vaginismus. This usually afflicts somewhat nervous girls and means that when anything goes near the vagina all the muscles in the vicinity go into spasm which makes internal examination nigh on impossible. God knows how she ever got pregnant!

So, I begin the examination and the vaginismus clamps down on my fingers making things very difficult (and my fingers increasingly numb!). At the tip of a finger I just feel the cervix.

She is six centimetres dilated, well on the way through the first part of the labour in the prelude to delivering these twins.

Only trouble is that she is only twenty-nine weeks into the pregnancy, which means that if they deliver now, the twins will be 11 weeks premature.

What to do now?

She obviously can't stay here. We need to transport her, and quickly, to specialist attention for both her and the babies. The regional centre, where her obstetrician is, does not have a neonatal intensive care, which is necessary for looking after premature babies, especially premature twins.

The nearest facility is in the capital city at the specialised obstetric hospital, which is two hours away by road. The town does not have a strip capable of taking a Royal Flying Doctor Service plane. So, we will have to make a two hours dash for the city before she delivers.

The good news is that we can give her something to slow or even switch off the labour until we get there.

I cancel the rest of the day in the surgery. Surprisingly or not, most patients don't mind too much as I think they know that one day it might be them requiring urgent, exclusive attention. Then off to the local hospital in the ambulance with the contractions coming every five minutes, each one concentrating her attention and raising a sheen of sweat on her forehead.

I insert an intravenous drip and commence a Ventolin (salbutamol) infusion. Now, salbutamol is a smooth muscle relaxant. Around about now, the largest smooth muscle in Anna's body is her uterus. The correct amount of Ventolin will cause it to relax and therefore 'switch' off the labour, at least long enough for us to get to the city. Ventolin is also used in puffer form, as many of you will know, for asthma. In that capacity, it relaxes the smooth muscle around the small airways and relieves the wheeze.

The only other thing I should mention about Ventolin is that it is a close relative of adrenaline, the body's natural 'fight or flight' hormone. Too much of it can make one's heart race, blood pressure goes sky high and can cause abnormal heart rhythms.

So, it is a bit of a balance between switching of the labour, or at least seriously dampening it down, and inducing these unwanted, and sometimes quite dangerous, side effects.

Well, here we are at the hospital. The medical student can barely contain his excitement at being in the thick of things and obviously thinking that this is the life and what country general practice is all about and almost striking heroic poses, jaw jutting, 'Hold the mirror steady, Sister' etc., etc. You know what I mean. All I'm thinking is bloody hell, how are we going to get out of this one!

I chat to the ambulance crew, all volunteers from the local community. We will need a pretty quick trip with no traffic hold-ups at the other end. We will need the rarely used Code Red!

What is a Code Red, I hear you ask?

The Ambulance Service has a priority system to designate the urgency of the task at the time. A Priority Three might be picking up a bed-ridden patient at a nursing home to go to a specialist outpatient appointment at the local public hospital. A Priority Two would be say, transporting a person with a broken leg to hospital. A Priority One is lights and sirens, flat out, where there is imminent danger to life or limb.

A Code Red is basically a Priority One with the added refinement of having a police chase car out in front plus the police manning of intersections to enable rapid, unimpeded transport of a time-critical patient.

Let's face it, Anna qualifies admirably. Potentially three lives are at risk.

Thankfully in those days, things like a Code Red was fairly easy to organise. A doctor just asked for it and it happened. Now it is more difficult with many more stakeholders, which can lead to critical delays before official permission is granted.

Whichever way you look at it, it puts a lot of responsibility on the doctor's shoulders to call things right and not unnecessarily mobilise the large amount of resources needed.

Anyway, off we set for the capital, two hours away.

In the front are the two volunteer ambulance officers. In the back are myself, the over-excited medical student, a midwife from our hospital (thank god, for her as I fear the student will be of little use), two delivery bundles (each containing the instruments and drapes for the delivery of one baby), the thermo cot (a thermostatically controlled heated cot in case the babies deliver in transit) and most importantly Anna with babies *in situ* and her Ventolin drip. And if you got the impression Anna was nervous before, the poor girl looks absolutely terrified now.

We also have her connected to a heart monitor to keep an eye on any unwanted or unpleasant side effects from the Ventolin.

Off we go!

When travelling on a Priority One, the ambulance was at that time required to have both the flashing lights and the siren on. After ten minutes of 'He-haw-he-haw', believe me you can hardly hear yourself think. The ambos are great though and at my request turn the siren off while not passing through towns or encountering traffic. Blessed silence!

The next town is 20 minutes up the road and is where we will pick up our police escort. We arrive and the police car, lights and sirens, screeches out in front of us and we continue. Everyone loves a good fast blast up the road and I am wondering if the two police out in front are in a similar over-excited state as the medical student.

As to the medical student, unfortunately the exciting times of country general practice have receded somewhat as he has been overcome by carsickness. Bouncing about in the back of an ambulance, and those old Ford ambulances had appalling suspension, has coloured him a delicate shade of green. To give him due credit however, he is still helping look after Anna.

And, how is Anna going in all this? She is tolerating the journey remarkably well. The only problem is that when I turn up the Ventolin infusion sufficiently high so as to turn off her contractions, her heart rate goes sky high and she has a number of funny heart rhythms, which generally are not considered a good thing. So, the Ventolin gets turned down, the heart improves but the contractions start again. So, the Ventolin gets turned up again. Back and forth. Eventually we get to some sort of equilibrium where the contractions subside to a dull roar and the heart reaction to the *Ventolin* is tolerable.

Outside, our cavalcade is now approaching the outskirt suburbs of the capital. More traffic and traffic lights and even a couple of railway lines to cross. Our progress so far, through a number of small country towns has been a breeze compared to the last bit of the journey coming up.

Incredibly, all is well. I don't know how they did it but every traffic light is manned by one or two police. We sail through, barely checking. We come to the railway line, there are police there and as we weave through the lowered barriers at their waved command, I look up the line. They have even stopped the train!

There are thirty-two traffic lights between the outskirts and the obstetric hospital. Each one is manned. Each one barely checks us. What an incredible performance by the Police Force! A great feeling to think that we are all focussed on doing the best for Anna and her unborn twins. Any other consideration is secondary.

We finally deliver Anna, babies inside, heart rate and rhythm reasonable, to her destination, but not without one further element of farce.

On the freeway, just below the parliament house the ambulance runs out of petrol!

We just stop. It was faintly amusing with an element of the ridiculous to see the leading police car, which for so long had been tearing along in front of us, hesitantly backing down the freeway off ramp we were due to take to see what had happened to us. Its lights still flashing heroically.

Anyway, our ambos get onto the ambulance dispatcher pretty quick smart. I am not too worried as Anna has settled, her contractions have ceased and her heart rate and rhythm have stabilised.

Another ambulance arrives next to us on the off ramp. In it is some poor guy who has broken his arm on a building site.

A light rain is falling. He is bundled out of his nice warm ambulance into ours, which is also warm but going nowhere. We pinch his ambulance and off we go again. The guy with the broken arm, despite his pain, calls, 'Good Luck'.

We have achieved what we set out to do. With great cooperation from the Police, the Ambulance Service and even the guy with the broken arm, we have delivered a twenty-nine-week pregnant mum with twins to definitive care at the major obstetric hospital for the state.

The twin girls are delivered by caesarean section later that day. They are eleven weeks premature and weigh about a kilo each. About the size of a large tub of butter!

The girls do well. Because of their prematurity, they stay in the Neonatal Intensive Care for quite a while but eventually come home and thrive.

I think the last time I saw them, they were about six years old. They came in to see me with their mother, holding hands and looking at me gravely, shyly, out of prominent googly eyes.

I didn't do any blood tests for thyroid function!

The Spleen

The spleen is an interesting organ.

It has been written about for years by such luminaries as Shakespeare in Julius Caesar "You shall digest the venom of your spleen…", describing Cassius' irritable nature. Eighteenth century authors similarly used the spleen as a descriptive for someone of 'irritable and uncertain temper' and 'hypochondriacal and hysterical affections'.

The French thought it was the source of pensive sadness and melancholy.

On a more cheerful note, the Ancient Greeks and the Talmud felt it was more related to happiness and laughter.

Whatever the origins and the interpretations placed upon it by the ancients, it was definitely felt to be part of emotion, good or bad.

But, I hear you ask, what has this got to do with anything? And, what does the spleen do anyway and particularly what has it got to do with this particular story?

Let me explain.

Those Monty Python fans will remember the liver being described as a '…large glandular organ in your ab-do-men'. (Meaning of Life, Live organ donation).

The spleen is also a 'glandular organ in your ab-do-men', but smaller and on the other side compared to the liver. It hides under the left lower ribs, which in most cases protect it from harm (the 9th, 10th and 11th left ribs).

It is purply-brown in colour and quite friable and fragile, being protected by a reasonably strong connective tissue capsule.

It has two main functions. The first one is, it is an important part of the immune system and it has been described as the biggest lymph node in the body.

The second, and the one we are mainly interested in for the purposes of this story, is its role in red blood cell storage and destruction.

It destroys old red blood cells at the rate of two or three million per second and to do this it receives something in the order of five to ten per cent of the blood flow coming from the heart each minute.

What I want to talk about today is what happens when the spleen is damaged in some sort of trauma.

This is generally considered a bad thing as having such a good blood supply it bleeds profusely and if the capsule is torn the bleeding doesn't tend to stop easily.

The other problem is that often injuries to the spleen are from blunt trauma (rather than a penetrating injury) and so bleeding from a 'ruptured' spleen tends to be internal bleeding which is not readily apparent sometimes until the patient (if they weren't a patient before they certainly will be by now) collapses from blood loss.

In ancient times, where the spleen became enlarged if a person had malaria (pre-treatment days) it would protrude out from its protective bony rib cage. Unkind people, or should we say assassins, knew this and would hit the person in that area with a metal rod, rupturing the spleen and causing fatal bleeding. Nice, ay!

Fortunately these days, thanks to sophisticated ultrasound capabilities in most Emergency Departments, this can be relatively easily detected in experienced hands. A problem may arise in rural and remote settings where this equipment is not necessarily easily accessible. There one has to rely entirely on one's clinical acumen.

A person can survive quite happily without their spleen once removed but it is good to preserve it if possible. Generally this can be done if the tough outer capsule is intact but if not, it often has to be removed.

One of the problems that occurs in people who have had their spleen removed is that they are prone to certain types of infection which can be quite nasty and overwhelming. This can be minimised by the judicious use of immunisation and antibiotics.

The stories I want to relate to you are about three such occasions where there was splenic injury without any sophisticated equipment being available.

The Clydesdale

Like many small country towns, the town where I lived and worked had an annual agricultural show. Produce and animals were displayed and judged. Trophies were awarded to the fortunate few and the unfortunate majority bemoaned their perceived failures and muttered darkly about the winners. The cake section was particularly vicious in that regard.

Great fun for all the community and was one of the highlights of the year for the town.

A big part of the proceedings was the horse section. Many came to ride in dressage and jumping events and display their equine protégés in the best turned out classes. Draught horses often would give displays of ploughing etc.

I don't know if you have ever seen a Clydesdale horse. They are huge and in the pre-motorised days were used extensively in agriculture for ploughing and in the cities to pull beer barrel drays and fire engines.

On this occasion, a very pleasant and popular local woman had brought her two lovingly cared for Clydesdales to display at the show.

She was engaged in unloading the first one from her truck but unfortunately the unloading ramp (the tailgate of her truck) was quite unsuitable and very steep.

The poor horse was tentatively starting down this ramp when it decided that it didn't like it one little bit and leapt the rest of the way to the ground.

This in itself would have been okay but the owner was in the way and the horse landed on her. She had fallen backwards

and the horse hoof, the size of a large dinner plate landed –
you guessed it – on the left side of her abdomen and lower left
rib cage.

I was at the show and was called for over the public
announcement system (this was pre-mobile phone days).

When I got to her, she was pale and sweaty (not a good
sign), in considerable pain with a rapid pulse and low blood
pressure. There was a large purpling bruise where the hoof
had landed on the left side of her abdomen and lower chest.

Fortunately the local ambulance was also at the show, so
we loaded her onto it, put in an intra-venous line and took her
to the regional hospital (fifty kilometres away) as quickly as
possible with me along for the ride.

The surgeon confirmed our suspicions that she did indeed
have a ruptured spleen and had lost quite a bit of blood,
unseen, into her abdomen.

Thankfully, they were able to remove the spleen, give her
a blood transfusion and she subsequently made a full
recovery.

I often reflect on how one minute everything is going
along quite normally, as it should and then suddenly, out of
the blue, things change and one is faced with a life-threatening
situation.

Luckily, in this case all was well.

The Aluminium Belt Line

In the hills behind our town, bauxite (the precursor ore to
making aluminium) had been discovered in large quantities
and was mined in an open cut manner and then transported by
a large covered conveyor belt line, quite a distance, to the
local refinery.

Alongside the belt line there was a service road, often
quite rough gravel, to enable crews to service and repair the
belt when required. It was a favourite track for motorbike
riders and particularly popular with city riders during the
weekends. It goes without saying that the company running
the mine was not happy with this and had frequent patrols to
discourage its use but many riders evaded discovery.

I was in my town surgery one afternoon when a call came in from the local ambulance that someone had had a motorbike accident on the belt line, some thirty kilometres away, and could I please come out there straight away, as the rider was not in good condition.

The town ambulance had already been alerted and the volunteer ambos heading in from work and home to pick up the ambulance from the depot and head out there.

The shire ranger came by the surgery and offered to take me out to the scene, an offer I gladly accepted.

The police were also alerted.

Off we went and soon were on the gravel roads in the bush east of town. The ranger was a very experienced local bushman and an expert at driving on the tricky ball-bearing gravel roads – roads which I might add are beloved of rally drivers the world over.

Suddenly a police car roared past us, driven by a rather over-adrenalised young constable, showering us with small stones and enough choking dust to mean we had to abruptly pull to the side of the road until it cleared.

When we arrived at the scene, the same constable approached us with something of a swagger in his gait and said I should have travelled with him as he got there much quicker. I fervently, but silently, thanked my lucky stars that I did not!

We found that there was a young motorcyclist, lying by the conveyor belt, the refinery paramedics in attendance.

He was conscious and complained of a 'sore gut' but the most obvious injury was a compound fracture of his left femur (thighbone). The broken bone was sticking out through a rip in his jeans – yuk!

This is a most unpleasant injury. First, very painful. Second, one can lose a lot of blood from a fractured femur (up to three litres, maybe more than 50% of your total blood volume). Third, but a bit later, it can lead to bone and tissue infection which may have disastrous consequences.

Fortunately, he seemed to have a good pulse and blood pressure. I placed an intra-venous line in his arm, administered some IV morphine and fluids and loaded him into the ambulance, which had by then arrived and set off for the regional hospital some fifty kilometres away.

I went along to ensure all was well and we arrived at the hospital with no further dramas.

Then off we went home in our ambulance – me back to the surgery and the ambulance crew back to whatever they were doing when the call to arms came.

I heard later that the bone guys (orthopaedic surgeons) at the regional hospital were very keen to hop straight in and repair the fractured femur and hassling the anaesthetist to get on with things.

Quite rightly, the anaesthetist was concerned over the fact that the patient was increasingly complaining of his gut pain which was steadily growing worse.

An ultrasound was done and, you guessed it, the spleen was found to be ruptured but on this occasion the capsule was intact. The decision was therefore made to manage the splenic injury conservatively which is a good thing if possible as it reduces the risk of getting odd infections in the future, the possibility of which I mentioned earlier.

He was managed in the ICU for three to four days, being closely monitored, the broken femur in traction and receiving large doses of intravenous antibiotics to counter the possibility of infection in the leg.

Once they were happy that he was stable in the spleen department, they then took him to the operating theatre and fixed his femur.

The lesson?

Never be distracted by the obvious (the nasty thigh fracture) as the orthopaedic registrar was. Always consider all possible injury patterns and especially exclude things like internal injuries in trauma patients before commencing any surgery, however heroic and necessary.

A ruptured spleen declaring itself by internal blood loss, dropping the blood pressure into his boots during an operation would have been a potentially life-threatening disaster.

Thankfully averted by a sharp-eyed anaesthetist.

The Canoe Course

In the hills to the east of our town were a number of dams. Initially the water was used exclusively for irrigation purposes but in later years 'stolen' by the metropolitan areas to provide domestic water supplies.

In these days of reduced rainfall, these dams don't always fill but that is another story and an argument for a different forum.

The biggest dam used to regularly let water out to travel down to the smaller weir on the edge of the hills which then released water according to the irrigation needs of the local farmers, into pipes and channels and ultimately to their paddocks.

An international class 'white water' canoe course was constructed at the base of the larger dam, which took advantage of these regular irrigation outflows and the idea was that it could be set so that there was a 'dial-a-river' achieving slalom water levels required for all levels of competition.

There was not always competitions and several canoe clubs regularly travelled down to our area for practice sessions. A nice little tourist earner for the town!

One weekend I was on-call and in the surgery doing the usual Saturday afternoon session when I got a call from the local hospital.

Apparently there had been an accident at the white-water course and a man had brought his friend in by private car who had upended in his canoe and hit the left side of his chest and abdomen on underwater rocks. He was in considerable discomfort and a bit pale and sweaty.

Of interest, they were both doctors from the metropolitan hospitals, one a surgeon and the other, an Emergency Department physician. The surgeon was the injured one.

They had been at the hospital for about an hour when the nurses rang me, which sounds an unacceptable delay given the nature of the injury.

Why this was so, became apparent.

The ED guy when arriving at the hospital not unreasonably asked to insert an intra-venous line and administer some pain relief and fluids. As one would imagine, he was eminently qualified.

Unfortunately, we had a rather hide-rule-bound Director of Nursing (DON) who, equally unfortunately, happened to be on duty. She was very intelligent and a member of MENSA (the 'club' for people with abnormally high IQs). Despite that, she had no 'horse' sense at all – in fact, we all found her rather tiresome.

She refused to allow the ED guy to tend to his friend who obviously had a severe injury with a potentially ruptured spleen.

The reason, the ED guy was not accredited to our hospital. Rules were rules and must be adhered to regardless of the seriousness of an incident – what a twit!

To say there was a heated discussion would be an understatement.

Thankfully, there was a senior very experienced nurse on duty and she calmly prepared the necessary equipment, fluids and drugs for the ED guy to do the necessary.

The DON was politely (and rightly) ignored.

When I arrived things had settled down a lot. The patient was much improved, his vital signs (heart rate and blood pressure) were good and the pain relief had made him feel a lot better.

The DON had stumped off to her quarters in a tizz and we arranged an ambulance to take the patient to the regional hospital accompanied by his ED physician friend.

He did indeed have a ruptured spleen, which had broken the splenic capsule, and he was operated on later that day.

The repercussions from the DON did not end there; a formal complaint was made by her to the hospital board. Thankfully, the chairman of the board was very sensible and, after hearing the circumstances, dismissed the complaint with an admonition for greater flexibility on her part in the future.

So, there you have it, blind bureaucracy vs. common sense but in the setting where any delay may have had dire consequences.

It is said, "Rules are for the obedience of fools and the guidance of wise men (or women)."

She was the former when she should have been the latter and, so being, stuck to the letter of the law rather than be guided by it, which might well have had fatal consequences.

So, there you have it – three spleens and three stories.

Remember to look after yours!

Turbulence

Turbulence is an interesting word. It has been used to describe many things and situations, usually indicating the disruption of the normal flow of things.

A 'turbulent career' means one with many ups and downs. Politicians know that especially well.

'Will no one rid me of this turbulent priest?' was attributed to King Henry II and said about the then Archbishop of Canterbury, Thomas A Becket. Thomas was 'troublesome' and 'meddlesome' and unfortunately for Thomas, four of Henry's knights took him at his word (but without instruction) and obliged the king by murdering him. It was unfortunate for Henry II also, as he had to do a long and uncomfortable penance.

Today I don't want to necessarily talk about politicians or murdered priests but rather of the turbulence that many of us are subjected to when we travel – air turbulence when flying.

In that context, turbulence can be described as a sudden change in airflow, a 'disruption of the normal flow of things'.

At high altitude, it can be caused by encountering a jet-stream flow, described as a 'narrow variable band of very strong, predominantly westerly air currents that encircle the globe, several miles above the earth'.

Turbulence can also be caused by thermal activity, hot air rising either from a very hot day or from cumulus clouds or thunderstorms (cumulo-nimbus clouds – abbreviated to 'CB' in the trade). A good going thunderstorm has huge up and down drafts of up to 100 miles per hour. It may literally rip the wings of a plane. Thankfully, these days, in-plane weather radar ensures that these monsters are easily avoided.

For many years, I flew retrieving patients from far and wide, with the Royal Flying Doctor Service (RFDS).

During that time, I encountered my fair share of turbulence.

The summer months are always a bit hairy when it comes to turbulence in my experience, especially when the plane gets below nine or ten thousand feet. The hot air just flings it about a bit.

On this particular day, we were quite busy with a number of flights planned to various parts of the state.

The first was down to the deep south-east area to pick up a patient with a broken leg. The airfield was about 20 kilometres out of town, so the local ambulance picked the patient up from the hospital to rendezvous with the plane at the strip.

As we approached we came through rain and low cloud and were bumped around a bit, as we dodged rain showers. We had two goes at landing, having to 'go-round' at the first attempt due to poor visibility. The temperature on the ground at the airstrip was 18 degrees Celsius. Rather wintery sort of weather.

All was fine and we returned to our base after a two-hour flight and were then dispatched to go some 1000 kilometres into the desert centre of the state to pick up someone who had a suspected heart attack.

What a contrast in weather for the same state and same day!

The ground temperature this time was around 41 degrees Celsius. As we descended below 'the magic' 10,000 feet mark, we were increasingly buffeted by moderate turbulence which escalated toward the 'severe' end of the scale.

Despite having my seatbelt done as tight as possible, I still managed to crack my head on an overhead locker. Thankfully, coconut sore but intact. We all were very glad to get on the ground. Not fun!

The next incident that sticks in my mind happened a year or two later.

We had a call in the mid-afternoon to go to the south-east of the state (about an hour and a half away) to pick up a man who sounded very suspiciously like he was having, or had had, a heart attack.

As we walked out to the plane the weather was clear at our base but looking toward the range of hills to the east of us, we could see a number of thunderheads (CBs). They always look wonderful, castle like with multiple cotton wool battlements and turrets. Occasionally, we could see they were rent by lightning flashes.

They just look lovely but, hang on a minute; we are going to be flying in that direction very soon. Oh, bother!

Off we went. As we approached the hills, we were at around two-and-a-half-thousand feet of altitude with the cloud base on the thunderstorms another five thousand feet above us. Should be fine, we will fly well below them.

Fat chance. As we flew under the clouds, we started to buck, twist, rock and roll. We had strapped ourselves in really tightly but the 'ride' was incredible.

I remember, rather incredulously, watching my bag which had been securely strapped down onto the front stretcher in the back of the plane, gravitate forwards and hit the pilot on the back of his head. He was not amused. Neither, I might add, was I! The pilot was 'fighting' the controls and I looked out the window and saw the wings flapping energetically like a bird in flight. The plane was zooming and swooping just like a bird too. Oh, bother!

Thankfully, after what seemed to be an absolute age, we came out of the vortex and flew on, sweet as a nut, toward our heart man. I asked the pilot over the intercom if that was the worst turbulence he had encountered.

"Nah," was his laconic reply.

"I've been in worse, but I simply can't remember when!"

Thankfully the heart man was stable and we turned around for home base pretty quickly. You will be pleased to hear that we selected an alternative flight path to return on. We didn't really need to give the patient an unsupervised stress test. A stress test is always a supervised test where the patient is exercised and the ECG monitored to see if there is any problem with the coronary arteries, bit like running a car engine up toward the 'red-line' to see how it performs on the 'Dymo'.

The last story relates to a winter storm front.

We had been tasked to go to a regional centre to pick up two patients, both of whom had had heart attacks, and take them to a metropolitan hospital for further investigation and definitive treatment not available in the bush. Besides the pilot, there was a flight nurse and myself to ensure both patients could have the undivided attention of one clinical team member.

The storm front was due to hit the area around midday. As the flight was an hour and a bit each way, we would be in plenty of time to be back safely at our base, patients on their way by ambulance to hospital, by the time it arrived. We therefore departed on the outward flight around 8 a.m.

We landed at the regional airport shortly after 9 a.m. and taxied to the RFDS hangar. Two local ambulances were there, each with one of our patients and we busied ourselves transferring them onto our stretchers and connecting them to our monitors.

As we were doing this, I looked outside of the hangar and saw this wall of rain bearing down on us. The wind accompanying it was whipping up the dust on the nearby farm paddocks and reducing visibility considerably. Like a Sahara sandstorm. Here comes the front – early too!

Cursing the weather forecasters (you know who you are!), we pulled the hangar doors closed as it hit us.

The sound of the rain and shrieking wind on the metal roof and walls of the hangar was overwhelming. We could hardly hear ourselves think.

Needless to say, we were not going anywhere.

After a rather cacophonous hour it seemed to abate. The patients seemed to be in good spirits, one making nervous jokes about not wanting to fly in this weather. We assured him that neither did we.

Finally, it had settled to a stiff breeze and, in consultation with our operations staff, we decided it was safe to leave.

The patient we put on the back stretcher was a pleasant sixty-seven-year old woman who had had her heart attack whilst playing bowls. She was also an insulin-dependent diabetic, requiring up to four insulin injections per day to keep her blood sugar levels stable. That almost certainly contributed to her cardiac status.

The guy on the front stretcher was younger and a grader driver from one of the more remote shires further inland. He was pretty overweight which undoubtedly was a factor in his heart shenanigans.

Anyway, we loaded them onto the plane and off we went.

We took off and climbed out through some scattered clouds, avoiding the largest of them. Within ten minutes we were well above the clouds and in clear air. Time to relax!

Reading the patient notes, the nurse and I found that our back-stretcher patient had not been given her morning insulin before departing the regional hospital. Bugger!

The nurse got the glucose meter and got up and went down the back to test her sugar levels. With that, we hit a big air pocket and must have dropped at least a100 feet.

The nurse was kneeling in the rear next to the patient and I remember being totally astonished to see her literally levitate until her head hit the ceiling at least four feet above her.

Smooth air from there but the poor nurse had a very sore head and more importantly neck. Thankfully, scans cleared her neck of any major damage but she had to take quite a bit of time off work to recover.

Needless to say, the patients were terrified even though they were well strapped down onto their stretchers. Thankfully, there were no more bumps in the road for the rest of the journey.

Once we had landed at base, I rang the coronary care units where the patients were to be admitted. After giving the receiving doctor an update on their respective conditions plus an expected time of arrival (ETA), I informed him that there was no need to do a stress test as we had already done one on the way down from the bush!

So, when I fly sometimes inter-state or overseas with my wife, who hates any kind of turbulence and shudders at the slightest bump, I say:

"Nah, I've been in worse and I *can* remember when!"

Procidentia

Many, many moons ago, not quite when dinosaurs roamed the earth (but it sometimes feels like it on cold mornings!), I was a newly minted fourth year medical student. This was the first time we were actually let loose on an unsuspecting public.

That is not quite as bad as it sounds, as we were very junior and closely mentored and watched. I was part of a group of about six students assigned to a ward at one of the major teaching hospitals for a term in General Medicine. We knew nothing, though some of us thought we might, and wore short white coats indicators of our lowly status with stethoscopes nonchalantly but deliberately draped around our necks or hung out of our coat pockets.

However silly and ill-informed we may have been, it was still great to, at last, get away from the lecture theatres and into clinical medicine.

We were attached to a general medical team with two consultants (medical specialists), one registrar (a medical specialist in training), a senior medical officer (two or three years out) and an intern (first year out of medical school). Then, there were us.

Our medical team looked after about thirty patients with various problems. Once a week, the team was on 'take' which meant that for that particular day, any medical admissions entering the hospital via the Emergency Department, were looked after on our ward by our team.

Each student was assigned to 'look after' (given our total lack of any experience and precious little medical knowledge, I use that phrase in the loosest possible context!) a particular ward patient as they were admitted and during their in-patient stay.

We would take a medical history from the patient, a long and laborious task for both, and then do an examination to try to work out some sort of diagnosis and then what to do. This was known as 'clerking' a patient.

Thankfully for the patient, and I suspect also for us, this had already been done and dusted by the senior members of the team. Our tentative, frequently erroneous and sometimes bizarre, diagnoses did little or no harm to anyone except to further batter our bemused and fragile medical egos.

We also used to be given tutorials by the senior team members in a little room behind the nurses' station about half way down the ward from its entrance. It was a great feeling to be able to discuss and theorise about real cases and people who were on the ward, rather than learning only from textbooks.

On a board in our tutorial room, there was a list of patients being 'clerked' by each medical student, added to on take day and deducted from when they went home.

On this particular day, our team was on take and this continued from 8 a.m. until 10 p.m.

We were up on the ward just finishing off for the evening, when the alarm went off in one of the patient rooms.

Two of us rushed down there (myself and another medical student whose patient they were) plus the intern, who on later reflection had medical knowledge only marginally surpassing our own!

The patient was a dear old, Mediterranean grandmother (Nona), who had endeared herself to everyone with her bright personality, sense of fun and the wonderful pastries she got her family to make for the staff. I cannot remember now what her admission was for, but she was supposed to be going home within the next few days.

She was lying on the bed, gasping for breath, semi-conscious and with what appeared to be some blood on the sheets below her waist.

The intern, after closing the curtains around the bed, tentatively pulled back the sheet to see what had happened.

Unfortunately, she had suffered a total prolapse of her uterus, which meant that all of the womb was now sticking out through her vulva. This is called procidentia. Ghastly!

Thankfully, we don't see this all that much these days as gynaecology has come a long way but Nona had had multiple pregnancies and deliveries whilst still living in her village of origin in the 1930s and '40s. Obstetric care was, at best, basic and often it was back to work within a few hours of birth. This meant that her pelvic floor wasn't much to write home about and she had had some minor form of prolapse for many years.

On this occasion, there was a total prolapse of the whole womb, not just down a bit but right out onto the bed. For no obvious reason. A good cough can do it.

When this happens, it causes a massive autonomic nervous discharge via the para-sympathetic nerves, which slows the heart rate down dramatically and in some cases, stops it entirely.

As I found out later, the treatment is to immediately replace the uterus in its correct anatomical position, using a gloved hand to push the whole thing back up inside. Gruesome, but lifesaving. Unfortunately, back then we didn't have a clue. Neither, might I add, did the intern.

Nona's heart rate was taken (we had only just learnt to do this properly) and found to be around thirty beats per minute – not good.

The intern said we should do an ECG (Electro-Cardio-Graph). The reason for this escapes me but none of us knew any better so we helped prepare for the ECG.

Today an ECG is simple to do. There are sticky dots that are placed on the chest, the ECG connected by clips and the reading done, all in a minute or two.

Then there were suction cups. A small dollop of electrode gel was placed where each cup was to be put, the suction cups attached by squeezing the bulb of the cup and then 'suckering' it onto the skin. It takes forever and the bloody cups are always falling off and needing to be reapplied.

For poor old Nona, it was doubly hard with all of us fluffing around, the cups falling off, all of us getting in the way and the final bit of black farce was when my student colleague knelt on the bed to reapply a detached cup and squashed the large tube of electrode gel with his knee.

This went everywhere. All over the bed, all over us and, more appallingly, all over Nona.

The ECG, when finally taken, just showed us what we already knew. That was that Nona's heart rate was perilously low.

Finally, and thankfully, the registrar arrived, took in the situation at a glance, quickly put on a pair of gloves and pushed the uterus back to where it should be.

Sadly, by this time, Nona's heart had indeed stopped and despite prolonged CPR, led by the very competent registrar, she died.

We were totally devastated.

This was our first brush with actual death, which we had been intimately involved, someone we knew and liked, and indeed someone we had been (in theory anyway) responsible for. We had 'failed'.

We trudged back to the tutorial room behind the nurses' station, went in and closed the door. My colleague, whose patient she was, went to the board where the patient list was, and deliberately and very glumly crossed out her name. His pen made a lonely scratching type of noise.

With that, we both burst into peels of hysterical laughter.

There was nothing remotely amusing or funny about this ghastly situation but there was so much tension for all of us associated with the whole scenario that it was released only in this bizarre fashion.

Just then, we noticed the previously summoned family walking sombrely past the nurses' station toward Nona's room. Thankfully, the tutorial room door was closed and they heard nothing.

I have often thought about Nona and what happened that night and our reactions to it.

To some extent those involved in medicine (and this includes a broad range of different professionals) have to be somewhat inured to the daily tragedies they have to be involved in and face. Otherwise they would not be able to function.

Ours is a caring profession and what I like about it is that it is okay to care.

We all have to build a degree of a shield to dreadful, sad things, lest they might destroy us. On the other hand, we mustn't construct too much of a carapace or we will be hard and uncaring (unfortunately I know a few people like that), 'safe' but untouchable – a fine balance.

We use humour, often quite black, as a trigger for tension release and as a coping mechanism. Debriefing with colleagues who have faced the same things is enormously helpful. In my view counselling with a non-medical person is of little value and often offers meaningless platitudes of no practical use.

So that is my story of Nona and her procidentia. She was a beloved wife, mother and grandmother. She was greatly loved by many.

I think of her often, tell the cautionary tale of what happened and thank her for her life.

The Jesus Story

Have you ever heard of, or even had, a 'Jesus' moment or story?

I'm not talking about an involuntary exclamation of blasphemy like when, say, you hit your thumb with a hammer when performing some difficult or simple piece of carpentry.

That's not what I am on about.

What I mean by having a 'Jesus' moment is that something happens which defies normal rational explanation and reveals that there just may be someone up there looking after us however flawed we are.

God knows that I am not religious. I had that drummed out of me at school years ago when we had to go to church at least once a day and listen to a series of very ordinary, uninspiring priests wreck what seemed to be quite a good idea at the time.

The more I think about things, the more I feel that there is more in heaven and earth than can be explained by scientific rationalism.

These next two stories happened to me over my professional life. They probably do have some simple explanation but I like to think of them as a slight, almost imperceptible movement of the veil that separates us from who knows what, enabling the tiniest hint of a glance beyond it.

The first happened in Africa in 1999 and the second in Australia in 2007.

Let me tell you what occurred.

AFRICA 1999.

In 1999, I had the great good fortune to spend a year working as the Team Doctor for one of the World Rally

Teams based in Europe. During that year, I travelled with the team all over the world.

One of the most interesting places, where I spent a month, was a country in Africa.

At that time World Rallying was at its peak with eight manufacturers fielding teams for the championship.

Our rally team went out to Africa about a month before the local rally – the African leg of the World Rally Championship (WRC) series – do some testing of our rally car. Most teams did this, which meant items such as tyres, suspensions, gearboxes, differentials etc. could all be tested in the country, under similar conditions, that the rally was to be held in.

We tested in two or three local sites but the nicest was at a lake, about three to four hours north of the capital

The lake itself was about 30 kms long (north-south) and about five to ten kilometres wide. We stayed in a lovely old lodge, around mid-lake, on the western side. The lodge itself was single storied with wide cool verandas. It was set about 200 meters from the lake with well-kept lawns, dotted with acacia trees, sloping down all the way to the water. Dinner was served each night on the veranda and we would watch the hippopotami graze on the lawn.

Magic.

Testing in rallying is done flat out, trying, as nearly as possible to replicate conditions that would be found in that country's rally. That way anything that can go wrong, will go wrong, including accidents. It makes it almost more imperative to have a doctor in attendance than during the WRC event itself.

In most countries of the world, such as Europe or Australia, the test roads are closed off and there is no public access. Not so in Africa. The roads beside having the local populace and their domestic animals crossing at any odd time also has wild game which needless to say pay no attention to anyone, let alone a rally car.

How then to provide for safe, flat out testing?

The answer, which sounds very excessive, is to have a helicopter hovering some 20 metres over the test car 'calling the road' and advising the driver as to any upcoming hazards. Example, 'Elephant 100 metres on right, dead slow!'

I spent a great two weeks sitting in the left-hand front seat of the helicopter or chopper 'calling the road'.

Early one morning, when flying low over the reed beds at the edge of the lake, we noticed up ahead what appeared to be a zebra lying on its side. As we flew over at about ten metres, the lion, which had been hidden by the recumbent but dead zebra, lifted its head up to glare at us. His entire face and mane were covered with and matted by blood from 'the kill'. Incredible! The malevolence in that baleful gaze was palpable and frightening even at a safe distance.

Anyway, the test road we were using started on the south end of the lake, went up the east side through some very rough country and finally finished on a fast stretch of road at the north end of the lake. A distance of some fifty kilometres in all.

During testing, we often would have to land beside the broken test car, especially on the rougher eastern side of the lake. Usually the mechanic and engineer in the chopper could fix things but occasionally we would have to go back to the lodge to pick up a replacement part.

Now I am sorry I have digressed a little but it is important to have some idea what the set up was to understand the story.

We had had a particularly hot and frustrating day with many breakdowns and numerous 'returns to base' to pick up parts. We were on the last run of the day and looking forward to getting back to the lodge for a beer and a shower (most probably in that order too!).

We were up at the northern end of the lake and had just started on the fast piece of road that led to the end of the test stage. Because the road was fast and the rally car could sometimes do over 200kph, the chopper needed to stay a kilometre or two ahead of it to stay in front.

Suddenly, in the distance, we saw a column of dust ahead on the road and quickly went on ahead of the car to investigate.

When we arrived, there was a Toyota tray-back utility vehicle on its side in the middle of the road. By the time we had made one circle of the scene the rally car had arrived and called us to land on their radio.

The occupants, still in the vehicle, were two elderly missionary nurses doing an immunisation clinic at a nearby village. They had been driving back to the nearest town where they were staying when they came around a bend in the road and encountered a local riding a push bike dead smack centre in the middle of the road. In taking evasive action, (successfully I might add) they had flipped their vehicle.

What made this incident so incredible is that in the middle of nowhere (and believe me this was miles away from anywhere) within two minutes of their accident a helicopter plus a doctor lands beside them.

I always like to think that if there is 'someone up there' then these are the people, practising practical, 'love thy neighbour' Christianity, that He (or She) would most want to look after. Perhaps, more so than the so-called 'Princes of the Church'.

Fortunately, they were not in too bad a shape. One nun, Belgian, had a fracture of the neck of her left humerus (upper arm bone) and the other from Ireland had a nasty laceration on her forehead that I stitched up later.

The mechanic and the engineer soon had the vehicle the right way up and drove it back to our lodge. We loaded the nuns onto the chopper after a sling for one and a dressing for the other and off we went.

During the flight to the lodge, the Irish nun leaned across to me and said.

"You are an angel in disguise."

I couldn't resist paraphrasing Winston Churchill and replied.

"Yes, but pretty effectively disguised!"

AUSTRALIA 2007

It was half way through a somewhat lacklustre morning in the Emergency Department where I worked. Mainly, routine cases but interesting as always.

I happened to walk down to the Triage desk, which is nearby the ambulance bay.

Suddenly, this large four-wheel drive vehicle screeches to a halt and a distressed man leaps out, shouting that his wife is unconscious. One look showed a woman slumped in the rear seat, so we grab a gurney, load her on after some difficulty extracting her from the car, and quickly wheeled her into the resuscitation area.

The history we get from the husband is that he was doing some errands in his car close to home when his wife rang saying she had the most terrible headache. At that point in the conversation she started to lose consciousness and make gurgling noises down the phone.

He raced home, found her lying unconscious but breathing in the driveway of their house, loaded her into the back of his car and raced to the nearest ED which was us.

In the resus room, she was in a bad way. She was breathing (but only just), her pulse and BP were okay but she was deeply unconscious and unresponsive with a GCS (Glasgow Coma Score which is a measure of conscious level, 15 being completely normal and 3 being totally unresponsive) of 4. Her name was Jill.

I was team leader for that resus and we put in two IV drips, took blood for analysis and then we made the decision to anaesthetise, intubate and ventilate her. This was achieved quickly and with a minimum of fuss.

What to do then? She had obviously had a cerebral event, which had rendered her unconscious. The most likely cause was a bleed into the brain either from a Sub Arachnoid Haemorrhage or some intra-cranial mischief such as a previously silent and undiagnosed brain tumour.

We then took her down to the CT scanner, no mean feat with an intubated patient and there it was. A large bleed into the substance of the brain which had more than likely come from the rupture of an arterio-venous malformation, an abnormal leash of blood vessels, in the brain.

Unfortunately, the outlook for anyone, who has a bleed into the brain and then becomes unconscious because of it, is almost universally grim.

Our hospital has no emergency neurosurgery service so the decision was made to transfer her to the nearest tertiary hospital and, as she was anaesthetised, I would accompany her in the ambulance.

I sat down with the husband and explained what had happened, that the outlook was pretty grim and we were transferring her to another hospital for further treatment. He was devastated and told me Jill was twenty-nine years old and that eleven weeks earlier had given birth to their second child (the other one was three years old) who was still breast-feeding. How appalling was that!

The ambulance arrived and we loaded Jill on board. Her husband, Rod, would follow with Jill's parents who had thankfully arrived and were able to support him.

The trip was uneventful and we delivered her to the previously alerted, highly competent ED team and neurosurgeons there. Then off we went back to our ED to continue our shift.

I rang later in the day to be told that she was still in the operating theatre and things were still looking grim. I rang a few times over the next few days and she was still intubated and ventilated in the ICU in an induced coma and the outcome was uncertain.

After that I lost track of her. Other cases and life in general intervened and I'm sorry to say I lost track of Jill's progress. I must confess that sometimes if the outlook is poor as hers was, I don't enquire too closely as I find it too distressing to hear that the result was bad and the patient has died or is in a vegetative state.

I was absolutely gobsmacked some five months later when Jill and Rod walked into the ED with their two kids to thank me for saving her life. How good is that! That sort of thing always brings tears to my eyes and a lump into my throat. It still does when I am writing this.

The story they told me was incredible.

Rod's best friend, a guy called James, had been killed in a traffic accident some 18 months previously.

When Jill was 'out of it', she was unconscious for about ten days, initially when we intubated her, then at the tertiary hospital, firstly in the operating theatre and then in the Intensive Care, the only thing that she remembered is having James as a constant presence. He comforted her, told her everything would be all right and finally told her it was time for her to go back.

During that time apparently, James' mother happened to go to a medium to try and contact him. She was told that he couldn't talk to her now as he was busy elsewhere, saving the life of his best friend's wife!!!

SPOOKY!

I have always been somewhat sceptical about mediums – the kind of thing logic dictates cannot happen but at a very basic level we all would like to believe a bit. Unkinder souls than me have accused them of preying on the gullible and the vulnerable.

Perhaps, just occasionally, there is one that helps us to pull aside the veil a little.

So, there you have my two stories.

What do you think? Is there something or someone else out there looking out for us?

Fascinating Rhythm
(Ba-De-Da-Ba Dum)

The heart is a most wondrous organ and has been much admired throughout the ages.

It was felt to be the centre of a person's being, the core of their soul. Feelings were felt here and nowhere else. It 'quickened' when excited, frightened or in the presence of one's beloved. The heart shape represents, even today, love and falling in love. A lover spurned is said to be 'broken-hearted'. I imagine it has happened to most of us at some time or other.

It was 'the happening' organ.

The ancient Egyptians felt that particularly and preserved the heart (and other organs) in canopic jars for use in the after-life.

That sloppy curd-like material from inside the skull (rather gruesomely scooped out via the nostrils of the thankfully dead person) was quite rightly discarded as being of absolutely no importance!

You and I live in a more enlightened era and know that the brain controls all and the heart is just a pump.

But what a pump!

If one does the maths, the heart from its formation (in the yet-to-be-born foetus) until we shuffle off this mortal coil (at an average age of say, 85) and working at an average of 80 contractions per minute, will beat approximately 3.5 billion times during our life. Try getting a windmill pump to do that!

Some people avow that each heart has only a certain number of beats it can do and once that allotted number is reached, it just stops. Interesting!

But let us look more closely at the heart and how it works and also have a bit of a talk about what happens when it goes wrong.

The heart has four chambers and two sides.

There is a left and right side of the heart. Basically, the right side collects blood from the body and pumps it to the lungs, while the left side picks the now 'gas exchanged' blood (carbon dioxide got rid of and oxygen replenished) from the lungs and pumps it around the body.

In the unborn child the lungs are not used, as the foetus exists in this lovely body temperature water bath of amniotic fluid. They get all their nutrition, including oxygen, from the placenta via the umbilical cord. Therefore, there are a number of bypasses which help the blood to go straight around the body rather than through the non-functioning lungs, but that is another story. Today we are talking about the heart after birth – the 'adult' circulation.

Each side of the heart has two chambers. The upper ones are called the atria (or atrium in the singular for those scholars of Latin). They are the collecting chambers from the veins of the body on the right and the lungs on the left.

The lower ones are the ventricles and are the main pumping chambers, the powerhouse of the heart. The right ventricle is relatively small, having to only pump the small distance from the heart to the lungs and against relatively small resistance.

In contrast to the right, the left ventricle is huge and pumps blood all around the body against quite a bit more resistance. It is responsible for our blood pressure and making sure all our various organs get the oxygen and nutrients they require to properly function.

Without a doubt it is my favourite chamber (yes, I hear you say, "What a sad life he leads if that's what floats his boat"!)

Anyway, onwards with the story!

The heart is a positive displacement pump, which means that when it beats, or contracts, it forces the blood out of the chamber into the arteries. One-way valves then stop the blood regurgitating back into the chamber it has just left. As the chamber relaxes it then fills up, ready for the next emptying beat.

This is in sharp contrast to the impeller-type pump (like, say, in a swimming pool pump), which has an impeller which rotates and imparts energy to the fluid. The faster the impeller spins, the more fluid is pumped.

Of interest is that some artificial hearts work on the swimming pool, impeller-type principal, which can be disconcerting for the recipients as all they notice is a constant low hum!

When our natural heart beats or contracts, a wave of blood leaves the heart via the main artery, the aorta. You may be aware that blood pressure is given as two figures, one over the other. The top figure is called the systolic blood pressure and is the one which is measured when the heart contracts (systole) and that wave of blood leaves it. The second, or lower figure is called the diastolic blood pressure and is measured when the heart is relaxed (diastole), filling for the next beat.

The heart muscle itself is most interesting.

Generally, there are two types of muscles in the body. Involuntary or smooth muscle which is found in areas such as in the gut and are not under conscious control and skeletal or voluntary muscles that are under direct control of the brain and are used for voluntary movement such as running, jumping, bending, straightening and generally existing in a mobile world. Oh, and I almost forgot, also for breathing!

The heart or cardiac muscle is similar to the skeletal muscle with one important and fascinating (well for me anyway) difference. Skeletal muscle requires stimulation by a nerve to contract and function, otherwise it just sits there.

Cardiac muscle, if placed in a dish with the appropriate nutrients, will spontaneously contract and beat. How cool is that!

This capability is known as 'Inherent Rhythmicity'. What a great phrase, just savour it again.

'Inherent Rhythmicity!'

Yes, it is official, I have no life!

One can imagine that all these cardiac muscle fibres, contracting willy-nilly, independently of each other will not get much coordinated pumping done. Sometimes this happens in the operating heart and is called fibrillation. More on that later.

What is needed is something to make them all work together, like an orchestra requires a conductor.

To do this the heart has its own pacemaker called the Sino-Atrial Node, located up in the right atrium. This is the first to discharge before each beat and a wave of electrical activity passes down across the heart, causing all the fibres to contract synchronously.

This wave starts at the top of the atria and sweeps down towards the ventricles. This enables the atria to contract from the top down and push blood into the lower ventricles.

This electrical wave then heads for the ventricles themselves but with some really clever modifications in the wiring.

Firstly, at the junction of the atria and the ventricles there is almost total electrical isolation with (usually) just one pathway which is the only way the pacemaker stimulus can reach the ventricles. Where that enters the ventricular area is called the Atrio-Ventricular Node which is a sort of secondary pacemaker.

Secondly, there is a delay in the passage of the electrical stimulus of about one or two thousandths of a second. This allows the atria to fully empty into the still relaxed ventricles.

Thirdly, there is some sophisticated, insulated wiring (intriguingly called the Bundle of HIS – sounds like a line out of Blackadder!) that takes the stimulus to the bottom of the ventricles before emerging to cause them to contract. As the outlets for the ventricles (pulmonary artery on the right and aorta on the left) are towards the top of the heart, this means the ventricles contract from their lowest point, upwards allowing complete emptying of the chambers into their arterial outlets.

Neat.

My apologies to you for rabbiting on about electrical activity in the heart but it does have a bearing on the tales I want to share with you later in this story.

Yes, the heart does run on electricity like the other muscles of the body but it basically generates its own. The brain does not directly tell the heart to beat all the time (that would be exhausting!) but can modify the rate at which the heart beats by use of various nerves and hormones.

The heart, like any other muscle or organ for that matter, needs a blood supply to offer it nutrients and oxygen and to dispose of its waste products.

The arteries that do this are called the coronary arteries and come off the aorta very close to its origin and run along the surface of the heart. They can only work when the heart is relaxed, in between beats (diastole). Common sense would suggest that when the heart is contracting during a beat (systole), that all the muscle is very tight and precious little in the way of blood can travel down the coronary arteries.

Well…what can possibly go wrong with such a great set up. The answer is, unfortunately, a lot!

What I particularly wanted to talk about today was, what happens when the rhythm of the heart is disturbed.

However, since everyone is terrified about it and think any chest pain is the harbinger of doom, let's get heart attacks (officially called Acute Myocardial Infarction or AMI) out of the way.

Sometimes, well if the truth be known, increasingly often these days the coronary arteries become clogged up with, what is called, plaque. This is principally formed by cholesterol and comes from 'bad diet'. That fact has led, as you are no doubt aware, to a positive cascade of dietary advice from all and sundry. Some good advice, and some with no foundation in fact or reality at all.

Anyway, most people agree that too much cholesterol is a bad thing.

The cholesterol deposits in the wall of the coronary arteries (and other arteries also) and eventually, aided and abetted by clot formation in the artery, severely reduces its calibre or completely blocks it.

Many heart attacks occur when the person is exercising and asking the heart to work a bit. If the coronary arteries are narrowed and therefore unable to deliver the increasing requirement for blood, the heart muscle is compromised and starts to die.

This is not considered a good thing!

Angina pectoris or chest pain of cardiac origin (derived from the Latin; *angere* – 'to strangle' and *pectus* – 'the chest') is usually described by those unfortunate to experience it, as a heaviness or tightness across the chest.

I have often asked patients if they have chest pain to be told. "No pain, Doc, but it feels like there is an elephant sitting on my chest!"

This pain typically radiates to the arms, left one in particular, and jaw and associated with profuse sweating, nausea and breathlessness.

I once treated a patient, when I was a very new doctor, whose only symptoms were an aching in both elbows. The clincher for me was that this only happened when he was digging fence postholes. He was a fencing contractor! A profession change in the offing, perhaps?

Angina isn't always associated with an AMI (or death of heart muscle) but may just mean that the heart is under pressure and its blood supply is compromised.

In the setting of an actual AMI, as discussed, a part of the muscle dies and therefore by extension won't work anymore. If a large enough area is involved the functioning is severely compromised and may indeed stop.

The worst effects occur when the AMI is in the area of the electrical wiring (HISS, boo!). This can totally disrupt the heart's orderly function and, lead to the loss of the 'pacemaker' which means that the cardiac muscle fibres just contract independently of each other (bit like an orchestra when the conductor suddenly drops dead) and they 'fibrillate' or just twitch a bit. Atrial Fibrillation (AF) one can survive but Ventricular Fibrillation (VF), unless corrected, is a game-changer and indeed a game-over scenario.

If the ventricle fibrillates, the cardiac output and out flow falls to zero which means the rest of the heart gets no blood at all and then dies, followed shortly thereafter by the brain and the rest of the body.

Fortunately, VF can be fixed (if one is lucky and quick about it) by external electricity in the form of a defibrillator. That literally 'shocks' the heart (which has a 'what the f…was that?' moment) and allows the natural pacemaker to reassert itself. With any sort of luck!

Early defibrillation works. That is the reason that so many venues, especially sporting ones, have readily available AEDs (Automatic External Defibrillators). Not necessarily for the athletes but for the sometimes over excited and, may I unkindly say, over-indulging spectators.

Anyway, if one is lucky enough to survive an AMI what can then be done?

Ideally what is needed is to restore the blood supply to the compromised heart muscle and allow those bits that are just 'feeling poorly' as opposed to having already died, to live again. The quicker happens the better.

A number of years ago, this was done by administering a clot-busting drug intravenously to dissolve the clot and restore blood flow in the particular coronary artery. This was called 'thrombolysis' (form the Geek and Latin: *Thrombus*' = a lump or clump and *'lysis'*– to loosen)

This was a game changer when introduced, but had a number of setbacks which included (in some people only) a tendency to bleed from various orifices as the body's normal coagulation ability has been temporarily suspended. In addition, as the clot is dissolved and the heart muscle blood supply is restored, there can be some funny (and quite alarming) rhythm changes in the heart's electrical activity, known as 'Reperfusion Arrhythmias'.

In major centres, cardiac catheterisation laboratories are now available. Using a catheter inserted in the groin (or arm) the coronary artery having problems is identified, the clot cleared and a stent (like a small tubular cage that expands once placed) inserted to keep the artery open for the future.

This is done as quickly as possible because, just like lawyers and accountants say that *'Time is money!'* the cardiologists say *'Time is muscle'* – the longer definitive action is delayed, the more heart muscle may die.

Sometimes, immediate intervention is not necessary and investigation and treatment can be done as an elective (meaning planned) procedure. Usually this involves doing the catheter type procedure again, identifying any blockage and placing a stent at that place.

Rarely, these days it is necessary to resort to surgery in the form of a Coronary Artery Bypass Graft (known as a CABG – pronounced Cabbage!). In this major operation the chest is opened up, a bit like a Kentucky Fried Chicken, and using veins harvested from the legs or arms (or sometimes arteries from the chest) the blocked portion of the coronary artery is directly bypassed by the grafted vein or artery. Unlike the poor chicken I alluded to before, you will be delighted to hear that in each case the patient's chest is restored to normal anatomy!

CABG is major stuff and while very successful, recovery time is long.

Hopefully, I have covered heart attacks and what to do about them to most people's satisfaction.

Perhaps, given this story is a bit long and perish the thought, a bit of a dry subject, it is time for a tale.

I was doing a locum at a country hospital, close to my old stamping ground where I was a rural GP. This involved a 24-hour stint covering the Emergency Department as the only doctor available after normal hours.

Around 10 p.m., I was called to the ED to see a patient with chest pain and most, if not all, of the symptoms we discussed earlier.

As it turned out, he was one of my old patients. It was good to see him and his family but I think we could safely say any reunion could have been under more cheery circumstances.

I put in an IV and gave him some *Morphine* whilst the nurse was doing and ECG (electro-cardiograph).

And…there it was. A rip roaring, 24 carat AMI.

You remember the *'Time is Muscle'* mantra, well we were at least three hours away from the nearest Cath lab but there were thrombolysing drugs available at the hospital.

We set up for the appropriate infusion and thought we were cooking with gas.

However, because of the availability of the Cath lab at my usual hospital, it had been quite sometime since I had last thrombolysed anyone, and I had quite forgotten about the dreaded 'Reperfusion Arrhythmias'!

I remember standing by the bedside, talking to his family, which included his wife, two adult sons, his brother and his wife, about what they had been doing and what my family had been doing since last we met.

The poor patient was drenched in sweat, grimacing and groaning in pain whilst his ECG rhythms looked like a paper version of 'the 1812 Overture'!

He was very hairy and I remember hissing to the nurse from the corner of my mouth to shave his chest, double quick, so we could apply the defibrillator pads, all the while keeping up the inane conversation with his family.

Time seemed to be frozen, the whole black farce crescendo-ing when…

Suddenly he sat up and said, "I feel GREAT!" I looked at the ECG and it was normal. The terrifying drug had scared the pants of me but had worked.

After that it was relatively simple to organise an evacuation to a metropolitan teaching hospital with a Coronary Care Unit. He had a stent inserted and went back to normal farming but agreed to slow down a bit and even eat the occasional salad.

Here endeth the tale!

What I mainly wanted to talk about is what happens when the normal electrical rhythm of the heart (called Sinus Rhythm after the Sino-Atrial node we discussed earlier) is upset. This is known as an 'arrhythmia' (derived from Old

English the 'a' meaning 'without' and 'rhythm' being self-explanatory!)

Arrhythmias can be fast or slow (heartbeat that is) and there are many varieties of each.

I just wanted to talk about two of them today. A fast, and a slow one.

The fast one is known as Atrial Fibrillation (called AF in the trade).

One can survive if the top chambers, the atria, fibrillate but not if the ventricles do. Atrial fibrillation, whilst not necessarily life threatening, can cause a number of problems.

The first is that, given that the primary pacemaker (the SA node) is not operating, the secondary pacemaker, the AV node at the electrical gateway to the ventricles, is bombarded by a whole lot of electrical stimuli coming from the random discharges of the fibrillating atria.

This means that the heart rate, driven by the bombarded AV node, can get very high.

The problem with that is that filling time for the ventricles is greatly reduced (remember the positive displacement pump) and the efficiency of the heart pump reduces significantly as the rate gets higher. The ventricles are already missing out on the coordinated contraction of the atria to help fill them. The other problem is that, as you no doubt remember, the coronary arteries only get their blood supply when the heart muscle is relaxed, so there is precious little time for that if the heart is beating flat out.

The second problem with AF is within the fibrillating atria themselves.

As the walls of the atria are not moving much (they are just sitting there, twitching and being generally useless) blood clots can form on them. Sometimes if normal rhythm is restored, these may flick of and go anywhere in the body but cause most problems when they lodge in the brain and cause strokes of varying severity. That can also happen when the atria are still fibrillating.

To stop this happening, most people with established AF were given some form of anti-coagulant, such as Warfarin, that delightful relative of rat poison. Not only is it hard to get the dosage level of Warfarin right but the poor patient often may have a bleed, either internally or externally, of varying seriousness.

Now at last, after all that technical rubbish (boring but interesting?), let me tell you a tale. Unfortunately, without a happy ending.

I was on duty in the evening at our ED and went to see an 89-year-old woman who had been brought in by her family with a reduced conscious state.

She was an active woman, living independently in her own home with her supportive family near-by. She was also living with long term AF and was taking Warfarin for reasons we discussed before.

When I met her, she was drowsy and generally incoherent and difficult to rouse. She wasn't able to answer my questions but didn't appear to be in any particular distress. The family said they found her like that, sitting in her favourite chair, when they paid one of their usual twice-daily visits. There was some blood on the bathroom floor, so they thought she might have had a fall. She had a bruise and an abrasion on her forehead.

I suspected that she might have had a problem with a bleed into the brain secondary to her Warfarin, coupled with the fall. The Warfarin level is notoriously hard to control as it reacts with almost everything else ingested (such as other pills, food and wine). Indeed, her Warfarin levels were quite elevated.

The CT scan of her head showed a large subdural bleed (a discrete collection of blood/haemorrhage between the brain and the skull). The pressure of the bleed was pushing on her brain and causing her symptoms.

As we had no neurosurgical unit available at our hospital, we transferred her to one of the main metropolitan teaching hospitals which did have such a unit.

They stopped the Warfarin and reversed what was left in her blood stream and when her clotting had returned to normal, operated on her and drained the subdural collection.

Post-operatively, she did well. She regained consciousness the next day (after a night in the ICU) and seemed to be rapidly returning to her old self.

Great...but fate had other ideas.

Because she was, quite rightly, no longer anti-coagulated because of her brain bleed, a clot formed in her left atrium and was fired off into the circulation.

It lodged in and blocked a major artery to her brain, causing a massive stroke.

Three days after her operation, she died.

Sometimes medicine, as life itself, can be a real BASTARD!

The second story was a slow arrhythmia and a happier outcome.

Anthony was a delightful, ninety-seven-year-old man. He had served with distinction as an RSM (Regimental Sergeant Major) in the British Army in a number of theatres during the Second World War, including the desert, Italy and finally in Germany at the conclusion of hostilities.

Upon demobilisation, he had married his sweetheart, Betty, and seeking pastures new and fresher than dismal post-war Britain, had set sail for Australia.

He had four children, seven grandchildren and five great-grandchildren. Unfortunately, Betty had died some two years before I met him.

Despite Betty's death, he carried on well and kept his house and quite large garden immaculate. He lived alone but with his extensive family close by and keeping a loving eye on him.

I was coming on duty for the evening shift at our ED and Anthony was in a cubicle, awaiting transfer to the ward. My colleague, who was going home to a well-deserved rest and possibly a glass of restorative wine, just said, "All worked up, nothing to do, just awaiting transfer to the ward."

He gave me a potted history on Anthony. Apparently, he had had a number of faints over the last month or two and had presented several times to hospital (ours and others) for investigation. Nothing was ever found to be the cause.

On this occasion, he had fainted (grandly called 'Syncope' in the trade) whilst he was tending his garden and fallen and hit his head. Again, extensive tests, including blood tests, ECGs and even a CT scan of his head, could find no abnormality. He was to be admitted for further investigations.

Fine. I could get on with seeing the first patient of the day.

When the patients are in their cubicles, many of them are monitored by an ECG, which is connected to a central monitor in the doctors' station. Having seen my first patient, I was writing the medical notes and happened to be sitting right next to the central ECG monitor.

The rhythm alarm went off on the monitor. This does this all the time and usually is the occasion of a quick glance and get back to what we are doing. Most of the alarms are patient movement, lead disconnection or some such artifactual reason and therefore can get rather annoying!

It was Anthony's monitor alarming. I glanced at the display and the ECG trace was a 'flat line'.

Right, I thought. *The bloody lead is disconnected.* I glanced across at Anthony and he was clearly unconscious!

As I leapt to my feet and was about to call to the other staff, the trace returned to the normal sinus rhythm we discussed before. With that, Anthony opened his eyes and looked bemusedly around. The 'flat line' lasted about seven seconds!

I went quickly to his bedside and asked him how he was. He said, "I'm good thanks, Doc, but I think I had another of my turns."

I'll say he had!

So, what had happened?

Anthony's normal main pacemaker, his SA node, was not working properly and cutting out on odd occasions for no obvious reason. This is known as 'Sick Sinus Syndrome'.

When this happens, usually the secondary pacemaker, the AV node, cuts in. That has a slow rate of about 35 to 40 beats a minute, so one doesn't usually faint but rather get giddy with exercise or upright posture.

For some reason in Anthony's case, his AV node had 'gone out in sympathy' and not worked either. This meant, no electrical activity or pacing in the heart and therefore no heartbeat or output for the seven seconds we observed. That will not just make you giddy but will make you unconscious!

I would love to claim credit for brilliant clinical acumen but sadly I can't.

I was just fortunate to catch the rhythm on the monitor at precisely the right time when it was occurring. Since it was happening only a couple of times a week, my colleagues, not unreasonably did not catch it despite close monitoring.

Within an hour, Anthony was fitted with a brand, spanking new internal pacemaker. He went home to the bosom of his family and his beloved garden and, last I heard, was still going strong.

Well, there you have it.

I hope you have enjoyed my story(ies) of this most fascinating of all organs and its rhythmic foibles.

I admire the heart above all of the organs, but then as I admitted earlier, I have no life.

Death of a Co-driver

In 1990s, I was involved in the local round of the World Rally Championship, which at that time was run out of our state's capital city.

It was run over three competition days in the forests and hills to the east of the city and also down in the south west of the state.

Several international teams had entered as well as national and state competitors.

The basic principal of a car rally is that there are a number of special stages, varying in length from say three to fifty kilometres. The roads are closed to the public and the cars start individually two to three minutes apart and race against the clock (not directly against each other like circuit racing).

At the end of some thirty stages, it is the car with the lowest elapsed time who is declared the winner.

Each car has a driver (a somewhat obvious observation!) and also a co-driver who reads the 'pace notes' which the two of them have compiled during reconnaissance when they are allowed two or three runs over the stage (at normal road speed) to make their notes. It is said that a good co-driver adds up to 15% to the speed of the rally car through the stage.

I was part of the medical team for the event.

Each stage has a medical car and ambulance at the start of the stage and in stages that are longer than 15 kilometres, further medical cars and ambulances at intermediate points throughout the stage – the number depending on stage length.

In addition, at that time there were two safety helicopters (Choppers 1 and 2) who patrolled the stages from above, made sure they were clear of the public and safe for competition. Also, one helicopter would follow the first few competitors through each stage to make sure all was well – this is called 'Zeroing' the stage. Choppers 1 and 2 took turn about to Zero each Stage

My role at the event this year was to act as medical officer in one of the two safety helicopters – Chopper 1. Another friend of mine, was the observer.

As we had Zeroed the previous stage (Stage 1), Chopper 2 was to zero the next stage and we were to set-down on the ground somewhere in the second stage to conserve fuel before moving onto our next zeroing stage. This stage was well into the bush in the hills east of, and about 50 kilometres from, the city.

We were looking for a place to land and thought we had found a nice spot for a bit of semi-authorised spectating and were told in no uncertain term by Rally Base (the Command Radio network) that this spot was reserved for VIPs and would we please go away!

So, we went further down the stage and found a good spot about half way through it.

We landed about 100 metres away from the course and set out to walk up to the nearby Road Closure (Any road that intersects the stage is bunted, taped off and manned by Road Closure officials to prevent unauthorised entry onto the course.) for a bit of spectating.

As we were walking down a little track toward the course we heard the noise of an approaching car at full throttle and then a big bang and no further engine noise.

We ran obliquely through the bush toward what we assumed was the accident scene, crossed a deep gully (with some difficulty), and then arrived at the car.

When we arrived at the accident, the co-driver was still in the car and the driver was out of the car under his own steam.

The car was inverted on its roof and bonnet. A tyre about five metres away was burning and later we found a spring from the suspension about 50 metres away. Obviously, there had been a big impact. Apparently, the car had been travelling at around 140 kph and gone over two smallish jumps, got out of line and side swiped a tree.

The co-driver was sitting on the 'ceiling' of the inverted car. He was still moving spontaneously at that time, helmet still in place, mike-jack still connected, blood on his face.

The Road Closure crew, thankfully, were trained ambulance officers and between us we got him out of the vehicle and shifted him some ten metres into the bush away from the side of the road.

He was speaking coherently but not all together sensibly – I remember him calling out to the driver, "What's happened, what's happened, are you okay?"

That sounded quite reasonable but he kept on chanting that phrase like a mantra despite reassurances that his driver was indeed fine.

He was obviously badly injured but moving his head spontaneously so we took off his helmet.

I undid his driving suit and felt his chest and abdomen. There was a lot of bruising and contusions over his right lower chest and ribs extending down onto his abdomen over the liver area.

At that time the pilot, who we had dispatched to get the medical kit from the chopper (we didn't need it to spectate!) had arrived back, puffing and red-faced having negotiated that bloody gully carrying a full load.

I inserted an intra-venous line and gave him some IV fluid. I distinctly remember thinking I had better not cut his driving suit to access his arm for the IV or I would be in trouble as driving suits are bloody expensive! Idiot!

At this time he was still conscious and coherent though a little inappropriate.

He then started to complain of shortness of breath and pain in the right side of his chest.

I was concerned about the possibility of a pneumothorax (a collapsed lung) so I put the largest IV cannula I had into the right side of his chest and got a very satisfactory hiss of escaping air, indicating that indeed he did have a pneumothorax.

He seemed to be breathing much easier having done that.

We then started, with him on a stretcher, to move down the course toward our helicopter. The dreaded gully would have been an insurmountable obstacle to the stretcher party.

I had sometime earlier radioed for assistance from another doctor who was in Chopper 2. For some reason there was no proper intercostal drain (to evacuate the air from the chest when a lung collapses) in our medical kit and besides I needed his assistance. He had to stop at the midpoint ambulance, some two kms away, to retrieve the inter-costal drain from their kit before coming on to us.

Unfortunately, there was no place to land close to the mid-point ambulance (there were lots of stumps in the way) so the chopper had to hover while he jumped out onto a stump, got the gear and then, not without some difficulty, clambered back into his chopper.

My medical colleague and his team arrived and caught up with us as we had left the course roadside and were going down the small track I mentioned earlier toward Chopper1.

During the journey so far to the helicopter, the co-driver's condition was deteriorating. His conscious state was becoming worse and he was coughing up more and more blood.

Once we reached the Chopper 1 we decided that because of his condition we would do two things.

Firstly, we would anaesthetise and intubate/ventilate him (my colleague is an anaesthetist) and secondly, we would insert a proper drain into his chest with a one-way valve (called a Heimlich valve) attached to enable better treatment of his collapsed lung.

We did that and felt we had slightly more control of the situation though the co-driver's condition was not good and we were all very concerned about his chances of survival.

He needed to be evacuated to hospital as quickly as possible. There was a large evacuation helicopter but that was being used elsewhere (for VIPs!) and was about 15 minutes away.

We took the door of one side of the rear of Chopper 1 (a Jet Ranger) and placed him on the stretcher on the rear seat. I knelt in the foot well of the rear seat by his head and used the ventilator bag to breath for him. On the other side of the rear helicopter seat his legs were sticking out the open door!

And off we took, headed for the city 50 kms away.

I can't remember a great deal of that journey apart from the fact it was noisy and cold – after all we were missing one door of the helicopter.

I do remember asking the pilot if he could go any faster and getting the reply that if we went any quicker the engine would blow up!

We went straight across the main runway of the international airport, having declared an emergency flight and I looked up briefly to see a Boeing 747 on final pull up and go around again! *Oh, shit!*

During the journey, our patient was not travelling well.

Each time I ventilated him with the bag, there was a gurgling sound and increasing amounts of blood were coming out of his mouth and up the ventilation tube and the chest drainage tube.

I thought at one stage he had died but then he moved spontaneously and I was slightly reassured.

We landed at the city heliport by the river. We were met by an old friend of mine who was a staff specialist at the Emergency Department of the main tertiary metropolitan hospital.

Together we applied ECG leads and determined there was little cardiac activity so chest compressions were started as the ambulance raced to the ED.

This continued once we reached the hospital and he was taken to the trauma room where despite full resuscitative efforts, a brief period of normal cardiac rhythm and a weak pulse, he died some 15 minutes after admission.

I was absolutely shattered. Once I came down off the adrenaline high, I was very emotional and exhausted. Obviously, that is nothing compared to what his friends and family went through, but it affected me deeply.

I somehow stumbled back to the Command Centre. People were looking at me oddly and I realised I was covered in the blood which he had been coughing up during the journey. Thankfully, someone found me some overalls I was able to change into and then talked to the Clerk of Course (the most senior official of the rally) and drafted a report which was sent to the FIA in Paris later that day.

I was not in a fit state for much but the Clerk of Course asked me to accompany the driver back to the hospital to formally identify his co-driver and close friend. Ghastly, but we got through it together.

Well, what had happened? What lead to the death of a much-loved husband and one of his country's legends? He was a well-respected academic and at that time held a land speed record.

The lateral attachments of the co-driver's harness were on the B pillar (between the front and back seats) rather than the roll cage. When they hit the tree, it took out the B pillar but left the roll cage intact. He was therefore wrenched on his right-hand side, crushing his chest, liver and right kidney. He had extensive internal bleeding into his chest and abdomen

The accident and subsequent injuries he suffered were non-survivable.

What did we learn?

We learnt that the medical equipment needed to be much improved although at that time it was considered to be equal to anywhere in the world.

We learnt that all the medical kits should be standardised and include the necessary gear for any foreseeable emergency intervention.

We learnt that we needed each medical unit, vehicular and aeronautical, to have good patient monitoring capabilities.

We learnt that there must be a dedicated evacuation helicopter tasked only for the rally and not diverted to any other task (like taking VIPs around!).

The next year my colleague and I took the driver's and co-driver's wives out for the day to visit the accident site, see the really nice memorial stone and plaque that the rally organisation had erected there and generally discussed what had happened and why it had happened.

There is no such thing as closure, but I think that this visit gave us all a little bit of comfort.

Jesus, His Brother and Me

Caterina had been widowed for about two years when I arrived in town. She lived on and ran a small farm about five kilometres out of town near the river, looked after her three children, a younger girl and two older boys. She got some help from relatives who lived close by and generally made a go of it.

Her biggest help, however, came from her dead husband with whom she conversed each night and who gave her really good pointers on how to run the farm and was for her a source of great comfort.

She would tell me this with an entirely straight face when she came to see me in the surgery to have her blood pressure checked, as if it was the most natural thing in the world when I asked her how she was coping with the kids and the farm. I once asked her if that was a strange thing to happen that her husband would speak to her and she looked at me as if I was barking mad.

I haven't mentioned that Caterina was a somewhat unprepossessing individual. She was stout – the unkind amongst us might have said fat. She invariably wore black widow's weeds. Her eyebrows met in the middle and she had several warts on her face, which sprouted long hairs. Her moustache was better than my one pathetic attempt at facial hair when I was 20. She didn't walk so much as waddle.

Anyway, back to the story.

This state of affairs continued for a few years. I didn't intervene. Why should I? Though clearly psychotic, she wasn't doing anyone any harm and indeed was functioning rather well in her various roles of mother, farmer and communer with the dead.

Over a couple of visits, one year, I noticed that she was looking at me strangely and sniggering to herself. On the second occasion, I asked her what was wrong but all she would do is look coquettishly at me, wag her finger and say, "You, naughty boy!"

At the next visit, I finally got to the bottom of it. Apparently, Jesus, his brother and I had been visiting her at night and giving her a good seeing to. The telling of this tale induced a paroxysm of finger wagging and chortling from Caterina.

I have always had trouble keeping a straight face when confronted with the ridiculous and this occasion was no exception. Unfortunately, I couldn't help myself; I broke into a broad grin and may have even had a chortle of my own. At this she said, "You can laugh, you dirty boy, after everything you did to me last night! And as for Jesus' brother, he is even worse than you." At this stage, I think I drew blood from biting my cheek to try and stop laughing out loud.

At the end of the consult, with me rendered almost helpless with poorly suppressed mirth, she got to her feet and waddled toward the door. As she reached it, she looked alluringly over her shoulder, arched an eyebrow, batted her eyelashes, gave me a wave and said, "See you tonight…don't be late!"

It was several minutes before I could compose myself enough to summon the next patient.

I was quite concerned with this turn of events. Needless to say, neither myself, Jesus, nor his brother had been anywhere near her farm, especially after dark.

Over the next six months, there were two or three further visits to the surgery. Though never as forthright as that first revelation there were plenty of inappropriate laughter and the occasional finger wagging. I finally managed to keep a straight face, but I was always somewhat relieved when she left the room.

Then one day it all changed. Her eldest son came to see me, most concerned about his mother. He said that she had begun to act strangely, muttering to herself and casting suspicious glances at everything and everyone including the family. Most alarmingly, she had started sleeping with a large carving knife under her pillow. Worse than that, she had started answering the front door with the knife in one hand, concealed behind her back.

I had visions of some worthy god-bothering sort, earnestly keen to bring the word of the Lord to all and sundry, getting 15 inches of cold steel in his chest when rolling up at her place. Clearly time to do something and sooner rather than later.

Her son said that she refused to come to the surgery, so there was nothing for it but that I would have to go out to her place.

At my knock, she peered around the front door in a most unfriendly manner but I was relieved to be able to see both of her hands. She grudgingly admitted me and at my request started to make me a cup of coffee. All the time, casting dark looks at me and muttering inaudibly to herself. Thankfully, the son was in the room but he was looking very uncomfortable. I asked how she was and she said, "Well you ought to know, you've been very bad." Unlike previously, there was no desire on my part to smile – this seemed to be getting much blacker than before.

She then asked me if I would like milk with my coffee and when I said, "Yes," she threw the whole carton across the room at me. Fortunately, she was some way away and so I saw it coming and was able to duck. It hit the sideboard behind me and burst. Milk went everywhere.

I got to my feet, slightly shakily, and thanked her for the coffee and told her I must get back to the surgery and that I would see her later. She let me go without demur.

The son came outside with me, tears in his eyes. "You have to do something about Mum before she hurts someone or herself." I agreed and told him that she would have to be certified and sent to a mental institution for treatment.

I don't know what you know about certifying someone insane. At that time there were two forms that had to be filled in. The first is a Form 3, which is filled out by the medical practitioner which commits the patient on an involuntary basis to an approved mental institution, usually on the grounds that the patient is a danger to themselves or others. This must be approved by either a magistrate or a Justice of the Peace, who then also signs the other form –Form 5; it is an order to the police to convey the patient to the approved facility.

These legal steps must be gone through before the patient can be restrained and have medications administered to them against their will. A rather stark and unpleasant process, not undertaken lightly!

With the forms dully signed and accompanied by a police car, I set off for the farm with the local volunteers in the ambulance. I had rung the son to let him know what was happening and that we were on our way.

We parked in the drive, out of sight of the house, and approached on foot. I carried a syringe full of Haloperidol, a powerful sedative, which I was going to give her intramuscularly.

The son opened the door to our knock. I have never seen, nor do I want to again, such a look of pure terror on anyone's face as there was on Caterina's when she saw us. She whirled around and dashed out of the room, howling like the hounds of hell had arrived. God knows they probably had, no one knows what was going on in that poor demented brain.

What everyone had thought of as a bit of a lark had turned into something appalling.

We found her cowering in the bedroom, sobbing on the floor by the bed. As we approached she screamed and launched herself at us. It took four grown men to hold her down to enable me to give the injection. After what seemed an age, but was probably only a few minutes, she subsided and finally started snoring.

It was one of the saddest and hardest things that I have had to do. There is nothing funny about mental illness. I guess if we do occasionally laugh about it, it is only to relieve the tension that we all feel when we deal with it. The tension comes from the fact that we all occasionally stand on the edge of the precipice and peer over. We are just more fortunate than some, in that most of us are able to stop ourselves slipping over that edge.

So, Caterina went off to the metropolitan mental hospital and life returned to normal. About six weeks later, she came back and appeared to be okay. She didn't seem to bear any ill-will to anyone and the various voices, including that of her husband had stopped. She returned to the farm and the family and all seemed to go back to normal. The only thing of note was that they sold the farm and bought another just south of our town. The new place was bigger and closer to Caterina's brother's place. By now, both of her sons had left school and were working the property. She still came and saw me occasionally but also saw one of my partners as well.

About six months later, I was delivering a baby at lunchtime in the local hospital. My partner rang and said that Caterina had gone off again and that she needed to be certified. According to the family, she had been missing her anti-psychotic medications as she felt she was now cured.

I suggested that my partner organise all the forms and I would join him as soon as I could.

When I got to Caterina's place, the ambulance and police car were parked in the drive. I went inside to find two police and two ambos plus my partner confronting a clearly terrified Caterina in her bedroom. My partner had the syringe.

He approached Caterina making soothing noises along the lines of, "There, there we just need to take you to hospital and make you better." etc. When he got close to her she launched herself at him and gave him a tremendous clout on the snout, which broke his glasses, gave him a bloody nose and nearly knocked him out. All of the rest of us looked at her and him in astonishment and the policemen burst out laughing, as did we all finally. Understandably, he was not similarly amused.

The inevitable followed and Caterina was sedated and carted off to the metropolitan mental hospital. My partner got a new pair of glasses.

That really is the end of the story. Caterina came back to town, this time on a long acting injectable anti-psychotic and she never had further problems.

She did however sometimes look at me strangely as if she was searching for some elusive memory, which thankfully was just out of reach.

Asthma
All That Wheezes Ain't Necessarily So

Asthma is a mainly childhood disease that kids grow out of, treatment these days is so good that it is easily controlled. It's frightening when it happens, but we've basically got it licked, right?

WRONG!

Asthma is a life-long condition for most people and children, whilst they may 'grow out of it', many still remain susceptible for the rest of their lives.

The main problem is that the death rate from asthma has not really improved in the last half-century. Frightening!

So, what is asthma and how do we treat it? Let's talk about that and then I'll relate to you some of my encounters with asthma over the years, most of which thankfully, had a good outcome.

Asthma is basically the narrowing of the airways in the lungs in response to a number of stimuli. The air going through the narrowed airways has to travel faster than normal (and therefore, requires more effort by the respiratory muscles), causing a 'whistle' or what everyone calls it, a 'wheeze'.

Airways are, of course, very necessary as they deliver air from the outside atmosphere all the way down into the lungs to the air sacs (called 'alveoli') where they are intimately associated with tiny blood vessels (called 'capillaries') and gas exchange (carbon dioxide out and oxygen in) occurs. So close are the capillaries and alveoli that gas exchange occurs in a few thousandth of a second. So thin and small are the capillaries that it is said, that at any instant in time, the amount of blood in the lungs is equivalent to flinging a cup of it (blood) over an area the size of a tennis court. Isn't the body so incredible!

There are basically two mechanisms that cause these airways to narrow.

The first is the smooth muscles that are found in the walls of the smaller airways. The normal function of this smooth muscle is to allow airways to open and close (a bit anyway) in response to the gas-exchange needs. For example, when we are standing up, gravity means that there is slightly more blood in the lower part of the lungs than the top. The airway muscles in the upper part of the lungs reduce the airflow there and increase the airflow in the lower part of the lungs. As there is slightly more blood lower down, the lungs automatically have adjusted the airflow to bring maximum air in contact with maximum blood flow to optimise gas-exchange. Neat!

In response to stimuli, those muscles go into spasm, causing airway narrowing and wheezing.

The other factor that comes into play is inflammation. Asthma causes inflammation of the airways themselves. This causes two things. Firstly, the lining of the airways swells, protrude into the airway space and narrow it. Secondly the airway wall, in response to the inflammation, produces mucous which further impinges on the airway space and, in some cases, blocks it.

So, what are the stimuli (or stimuluses for the non-Latin scholars!) that trigger things?

Cold and the 'flu', cigarette smoke, allergies to things like pet dander and house mites, exercise, cold air with a weather change, industrial chemicals at work, smoke from a BBQ or bushfire and some medications. Sometimes high emotion and crying can trigger an asthma attack.

So how can we treat asthma? These days this is principally done with 'puffers' or inhalers, for the more technically minded.

Firstly, we can relieve the airway muscle spasm. The puffer used is something called Salbutamol, a close relative of adrenaline (the body's internal 'flight or fight' hormone). Most would know this as Ventolin. This relieves the muscle spasm and wheeze by relaxing the smooth muscle around the airway.

Salbutamol is given as an inhaler but sometimes in hospital (or at home for that matter), we use a nebuliser where oxygen in bubbled through a salbutamol mixture (salbutamol and saline), creating a mist, which is easily inhaled. Easier than having to coordinate an inhaled breath using a puffer, which can be hard if one is fighting for breath. The use of 'spacers' with the inhalers has helped, especially in the acute situation.

Other smooth muscles that Salbutamol relaxes are the uterus where it is used to inhibit premature labour and in the walls of the mucosal capillaries in anaphylaxis, but those are different stories.

Secondly, we can do something about the airway inflammation. To do this we used corticosteroids (steroids), usually in an inhaled form (such as Becotide) and sometimes taken orally or intravenously in the form of Prednisolone or Hydrocortisone.

These steroid agents decrease the inflammation in the airways, reducing the swelling and mucous production. But the rub is that this may take 12 to 24 hours to fully work as things have to work at a cellular level and that takes time. Not much immediate use in the setting of an acute asthma attack. Thankfully, the spasm relieving salbutamol works within a few minutes.

Treatment, therefore, is a combination of the rapid muscle spasm reliever and the longer acting inflammation reliever. If you have ever seen an Asthma Plan (every asthmatic should have one), they talk about the 'reliever' (salbutamol) and the 'preventer' (inhaled steroid). In fact, the inhaled steroids are used not only in the setting of an acute attack but also to keep inflammation of the airways down and reduce the likelihood of a fresh attack (thence the title 'preventer'). Puffing frantically on the 'brown' puffer (steroid) during an acute asthma attack will do something but not for 12 hours! The more immediate 'blue' puffer, salbutamol, is the one for you.

In the 'old' days there were other treatments which have generally faded into obscurity either because they didn't work all that well or had unacceptable side effects. They included theophylline (given in a time consuming intra-venous infusion) and sodium cromoglycate (known as Intal), which was used for 'allergic' asthma in children.

As I have said before, "Enough of the explanation already, let's get on with the stories."

Just before I do, I want to say that there is not one group of people who are asthmatics over there and the rest of us 'normals' over here.

Asthma is a continuum. Anyone can get asthma if the stimulus is big enough (example, chlorine gas in WWI – instant asthma before the poor unfortunates drowned in their own secretions!). The so-called 'asthmatics' just require less to set them off.

The other thing that you worry about with the severe asthmatic is, that because they are working at breathing so hard, they get exhausted and eventually will stop breathing with obviously dire consequences. The converse is that as your treatment works and the asthma comes under control, the patient will often go to sleep. Until then, they are terrified and awake, struggling lest they die.

Anyway, where was I?

The first story concerns Maria, a young woman with a young family and a hard-working farmer husband. During winter, especially if she got a cold or a chest infection (asthmatics can be more prone to chest infections) she would get severe asthma and present to our local hospital at all hours of the day.

She would often present fighting for breath, with low oxygen concentrations in her blood and confused. The confusion came from the reduced oxygen going to her brain, which, as you would appreciate, is considered a bad thing.

I would often give her a salbutamol nebuliser with additional oxygen, whilst I fiddled around trying to put in an IV drip (she had dreadful veins) to start the theophylline infusion.

One time, the 'neb' didn't seem to be doing anything and I was starting to get very apprehensive as her condition was deteriorating and I hadn't yet got a drip in.

In desperation, thinking laterally, I gave her some sub-cutaneous adrenaline (as I said usually used for anaphylaxis and a great smooth muscle relaxant). Not exactly recognised as first-line treatment but it was 3 a.m. in the morning and she was getting worse.

By the time I got the IV drip in, Maria had improved dramatically, and as the theophylline started to run, she was sitting up and talking normally to me.

I learnt something that night and I must say that 'sub-cut' adrenaline has got me out of few tight spots since.

Maria's condition seemed to stabilise after that evening and she never had such a severe attack again (thankfully for her but also for me!) but it still gives me the shivers when I think of it.

Following on from Maria's case, as we discussed if one's oxygen levels are low enough cognitive (that's brain!) function is compromised and the patient can become confused and occasionally agitated and aggressive.

Bill was a bit like Maria, in that he had episodic severe asthma, usually triggered by a chest infection. On this occasion, he had contracted pneumonia which had made him unwell in its own right but also worsened his asthma. We had admitted him to the hospital a few days earlier, treated his pneumonia with intra-venous antibiotics whilst maximising his asthma therapy with salbutamol 'nebs' and oral steroids.

All seemed to be on the 'up'.

I got a call, when I was preparing to come to work one morning, from the hospital saying that Bill had 'gone off'. Apparently, he had become drowsy and then aggressive toward the staff and so they had taken it on themselves to sedate him with Valium (a common benzodiazepine sedative) to quieten him down.

In that aim, they were spectacularly successful and by the time we got there (in a hurry I might add) he was barely breathing at all and certainly not giving them any grief!

What had happened was that his asthma had significantly worsened over-night (as it often does) and he was confused and aggressive because of his low, low oxygen levels and not because he was being naughty! The sedation had so dampened down the respiratory drive coming from his brain that he was very close to a respiratory arrest and death!

Whoooopps! (Generally, you don't want to hear that exclamation in a medical context, especially in surgery!)

There was no option other than to intubate and ventilate (put a tube down his trachea and breath for him) Bill and then administer salbutamol down the tube.

This we did and then had to take him by ambulance to the ICU at the regional hospital and after a few days, infection and asthma under control, they discharged him home.

Needless to say, we had a staff debrief where we gently (it is of no use and counter-productive shouting at and haranguing people) pointed out and discussed what had happened.

It never happened again.

On that matter, everyone makes mistakes. Even in medicine. Those that say they don't (make mistakes) have two possibilities and one certainly. The possibilities are that either they are lying or have not seem enough patients.

The certainty is that they are idiots!

I have never been to a major resuscitation that could not have been done differently or perhaps better. The important thing is to learn from every patient interaction, good or bad, and carry that knowledge into the future without pointing fingers at anyone involved. No one really benefits from being harangued, belittled or having blame apportioned to them. Debriefing should be collaborative and constructive, not accusatory. I think that equally applies in any workplace.

The next patient also had a very rocky course. She was admitted to our hospital by another doctor who shall remain nameless, with a diagnosis of asthma.

Yes, she did have a wheeze but it had another cause. She had what is called 'Congestive Cardiac Failure' or CCF. The words 'cardiac failure' sound appalling and implies the heart is suddenly going to stop but really it means that the heart, for what-ever reason, isn't pumping as well as it used to. This means that there is a bit of a backup of blood upstream of it. 'Upstream' of the heart are the lungs and this back up of blood means the lungs get stiff and make breathing more difficult. Some of the fluid (blood minus the cells) spills into the alveoli (remember them) and sort of sloshes around a bit, making gas exchange less efficient and causing some narrowing of the airways and hence, a 'wheeze'.

So, the patients can sometimes sound 'asthmatic' and indeed CCF is also sometimes called 'cardiac asthma'. On the chest X-Ray, it can be sometimes hard to differentiate between the two conditions.

Anyway, this patient was being treated heroically for asthma with inhaled salbutamol, oral steroids and some antibiotics thrown in for good measure. All this when she really has severe CCF and needed some diuretics (to get rid of the excess fluid in her body) and treatment for that condition.

Unfortunately, the prescribed treatment didn't work and she deteriorated markedly over the weekend. Thankfully, one of our more experienced colleagues was 'on' over that time and after being called to see her, ceased all asthma treatment and immediately commenced the correct treatment for CCF.

That was in the nick of time as she was in extremis but she required quite a long stay in the regional ICU before she was fully okay.

Thank God! A near miss!

Again, I learnt from that experience – and that was never, ever adhere slavishly to a single diagnosis. Often you will be spot on but if the treatment being administered is not working, stand back, go back to basics and think again. Your original idea may have been wrong!

The last story is happier. It didn't actually happen to me but I heard it on the radio once when I was travelling between hospitals when I was a medical student.

It tickled my fancy and I still laugh about it to this day.

There was this delightful elderly doctor recounting some of his stories from his long career. Bit like this story but perhaps I am not so delightful!

In even older days, one of the treatments for asthmas was to give theophylline in suppository form rather than via an IV drip like we used to.

The doctor recalled that he was working in a hospital emergency department and was going past a patient cubicle when he heard and saw the signs of moderately severe asthma coming from the patient in there. Wheezing, working very hard to breathe, unable to speak and looking terrified.

As he was flat out with another patient, he asked a junior nurse to give this patient two theophylline suppositories and he would be back as soon as he could to check on things.

Upon approaching the curtained cubicle on his return, he was relieved to hear that the wheezing had almost stopped.

He opened the curtain to see the patient, puce in the face, hardly breathing at all, with one theophylline suppository firmly fixed in each nostril!

Having great difficulty getting air into his lungs anyway, he had had at least 50% of his upper airway occluded making the whole process that much harder. History doesn't relate the details of the outcome but apparently the patient survived.

In summary, asthma is still a dangerous life-long disease which should never be taken lightly especially, by the sufferers. It can kill and it sometimes does. Every patient should have an asthma plan and adhere to it however un-cool it might be.

Nothing is quite as un-cool as being dead.

The Bush Race
Meeting Tragedy

Bush races are an Australian, and particularly West Australian, icon. They are thought to have their origins in the first half of the last century. They started as a way for the local jackaroos (stockmen) to settle just who had the best horse and progressed to be a major annual sporting and social fixture for the district and the surrounding stations. It was not unusual for a stockman to ride for days, leading or driving a mob of station horses, to get to the 'meet'.

Sadly, they are in decline, like many other things in the bush but there are still a few genuine gems left.

The one I have in mind is just about as isolated as you can get: 500 kilometres from the coast and the nearest town of any consequence 400 kilometres in the other direction. People, family and station groups camp out for three days of races and *gymkhana*s, and a high old time is had by all.

I had occasion to go to this meet at the behest of the Royal Flying Doctor Service (RFDS) to be the doctor on course, mainly as required for the racing but also to give medical cover for the whole extended weekend.

Things were going pretty well until the second-last race of the first day. There had been a delay and a false start so the horses were taken back to the mounting yard for a second go at things.

Now the jockeys are generally amateurs at this meet but for people born and bred in the bush the 'amateur' is as good as if not better than a lot of the professionals that you see around the place.

One of the horses was playing up a bit and the jockey, a young local girl widely acknowledged as a fine horsewoman, was having trouble with him. Someone approached to help lead him out, and with that the horse reared up on his back legs, causing the jockey to slide off his haunches. The horse then backed into the mounting yard rails, crushing the jockey between them and its rump.

When I got there, she was in a lot of pain and lying with her hip flexed. It was obvious that she had either broken or dislocated something in her hip or pelvis. Hard to tell, lying in the dust, miles from anywhere. X-ray machines aren't too plentiful out there.

The important thing was to make her feel more comfortable so I put an IV drip in her arm, gave her some morphine for the pain and some fluid as it was a hot day and she was a little dry. We took her back to the RFDS caravan/clinic and called for an RFDS aircraft to evacuate her. Within two hours of the accident she was in a modern, well-equipped aircraft heading out for hospital. Pretty good going for the middle of nowhere!

I wish I could say that that was the end of it. A successful evacuation of a person injured in a remote location to definitive care in a major hospital. The truth of the matter is that it was not to be.

The patient was initially evacuated to the local regional hospital where it was found that the hip was dislocated, not broken. Good news we all thought as when a bone is broken it has to mend but if something is dislocated you can put it back in and, provided that the joint capsule and ligaments aren't too stretched, full recovery with a bit of physio is fairly rapid.

Hips can be very hard to get back into their sockets when they dislocate because of the very strong muscles around the area. It is not unusual to need a full anaesthetic and paralysis of all muscles to get them back in. This girl was very fit and so her muscles around the hip were particularly powerful. At the regional centre they tried to get it back in using ordinary sedation but were, not surprisingly, unsuccessful. A transfer to the metropolitan area was therefore arranged, as there was no anaesthetist at the local hospital.

Unknown to any one, this girl, who had never been in hospital in her life except to have her two children, had a problem with the clotting of her blood. There are a group of patients who have what is known as 'thrombophilia'. This literally means 'clot loving'. In practice, it means that the blood in her veins will clot more readily than other people. It is thought to be a genetic trait.

What happened is that due to the trauma and her immobility, she formed a large clot in the veins of her legs and pelvis. This is called a Deep Vein Thrombosis or DVT. The problem is not with the DVT itself but in what it can do. If big enough it can break away from the area where it is formed and travel through the veins toward the heart and lungs. It lodges in the next set of capillaries, the next narrowing of the blood vessels, which is in the lungs where the vessels divide into smaller and smaller branches. This is to let the maximum amount of blood be exposed to the maximum amount of air for gas exchange – carbon dioxide for oxygen, which after all is the function of the lungs. When this happens, it is called a Pulmonary Embolism or PE.

A small PE is not life threatening, but a large one is. It blocks the passage of blood through the lungs and everything stops. A massive PE is one of the few causes of instantaneous death, immediate 'lights out' with no time even to draw breath. A DVT followed by a PE is the cause of the so-called 'economy class' syndrome where people have dropped dead after a long flight. Actually, it can happen in any class. All that is needed is someone with thrombophilia and the prolonged immobility that comes from a long flight, say to the UK.

Our patient did indeed get a DVT, followed by a moderate non-lethal PE but with one further cruel twist to the story. Usually the PE lodges in the lungs and because of the narrowing of the capillary blood vessels is unable to travel beyond the lungs. Not so with our patient.

Let me explain.

When we were all foetuses inside our mothers, you will appreciate that we do not need or use our lungs for gas exchange, rather get everything from the umbilical cord and the placenta. In fact, the lungs are collapsed and have very little blood flow through them. Besides, the foetus lives in a liquid environment, bathed in amniotic fluid.

To avoid putting blood through the 'useless' lungs there is a hole, more a flap, between the right and left atria, the two collecting chambers of the heart. The blood from the umbilical cord goes straight through to the left side of the heart and hence around the body, bypassing the lungs. In the adult human, and indeed anyone once they are born, the right side of the heart collects 'spent' blood from the body and pumps it through the lungs for gas exchange and the left side of the heart picks up the 'renewed' blood and pumps it around the body. Once we draw our first breath and the lungs expand, pressure differences ensure that the lung 'bypass hole' between the right and left atria slams shut and thereafter there is no communication between the right and left sides of the heart. In most people, about 95%, this hole will scar over but in a small number of people this doesn't happen and the flap is held closed by pressure alone.

Unfortunately for our patient she was one of the few whose 'flap' didn't scar over. When the PE occurred, it partially blocked the outflow of the right side of the heart causing the pressure in the right side to exceed that on the left. This allowed blood flow through the flap which took large amounts of clot with it. The clot went around the body but caused most mischief by blocking the main arteries to the brain which caused an immediate and fatal stroke.

And that is how a relatively minor accident led to the death of a young mother.

Maybe when she was fifty, she may have taken a trip to the UK and suffered the 'economy class' syndrome. May be not. Who knows? But at least she would have had twenty years to see her kids grow up.

So sometimes, despite the best will in the world, a rapid response providing sophisticated aerial evacuation and medical care, sometimes we just don't win.

The Pupil Is Fixed and Dilated

I did my term of obstetrics at an outer suburban hospital in the mid-1980s. This was part of the GP training programme known as the Family Medicine Programme (FMP), which was run by the Royal Australian College of General Practice. The FMP placed prospective GPs in good service jobs such as obstetrics and anaesthetics around the major and peripheral hospitals of the capital city. The FMP placements were great but the programme wasn't. It seemed to be terminally confused as to its role and indeed the role of General Practice in the wider medical community. By all accounts it still is.

Anyway, by great good fortune I managed to get one of the better placements at the obstetric hospital. It was good for a number of reasons.

Firstly, the teachers, all practising 'obs and gynae' people were first rate. Secondly you got to do much more than in the major tertiary obstetric hospital. There, there were nursing students, medical students and other residents not to mention the registrars all competing for the available deliveries. At this hospital there was just you with the consultant as a backup. The only drawback was that two of us covered the entire unit, which meant a one in two on call. Long shifts, but great experience.

I had a great time there and learnt a lot. Over six months, I delivered about 100 babies including vacuum extractions; there is nothing like doing a lot of normal deliveries to learn how to do it right.

I also assisted at about 25 Caesarean sections and acted as surgeon at about eight. My teachers were very switched on guys who thought that if I was going to go to the bush I should be able to do a Caesarean in an emergency.

That then provided my experience to practise obstetrics and when I went to the country, I soon had a thriving 'obs' practice doing about 50 to 100 deliveries per year. One good thing about delivering babies in my town was that a regional centre was only half an hour away and had a specialist obstetrician, so if you got into trouble you could shuffle the patient down there fairly quickly.

I always enjoyed delivering babies. For the most part everyone is healthy and disasters were few and far between. Also, everyone was usually happy with the result even if the baby was the wrong sex or looked like the milkman (sorry Peter). Sometimes it was hard to stay up most of the night and then have to do a full day's work afterwards but we seemed to manage. The thing that finally did it for me was that after a couple of disasters I was always wondering what was going to go wrong next.

This particular incident, however, was not a disaster but a win.

Jane was the daughter of one of our receptionists, Jill. That always puts a bit more pressure on you not to stuff it up. She came to see me for her antenatal care for her first child.

Everything was going well and she was into the last few weeks of the pregnancy when disaster struck.

Normally when a 'mid' came in for review at the surgery, the staff would give them a urine sample pot, they would go off to the loo and the urine would be tested for sugar and protein. This was part of the regular screening done at each visit to detect developing diabetes, urinary infection and pre-eclampsia.

Anyway, Jane came in, one of the last patients on a full Friday and a weekend off in the offing. Off she went to the loo with her sample pot to do the necessary. A little while later, Jill knocked on my door saying, "Come quickly!"

I went outside and there was Jane looking somewhat bemused, standing in the loo with an umbilical cord hanging down between her legs!

This is what is called a prolapsed cord and, in obstetrics, is an absolute emergency. You will appreciate that for that to happen, the membranes surrounding the baby must have ruptured (in other words, the 'waters have broken') and the umbilical cord has gone out through the cervix in front of the baby's head.

Now the umbilical cord is the baby's lifeline, providing as it does oxygen and nutrients. Catch this between the proverbial rock and a hard place, say the cervix and the baby's head, and the vital supplies are cut off. Akin to standing on a diver's air hose. It can be fatal to the baby if only occluded for even a short time.

Bloody hell! What to do! I felt the pulse in the cord and the foetal heart rate was varying between 60 and 200 beats per minute – a sure sign that the bub was under pressure and not doing too well.

First thing is to hold the baby's head off the cervix and the cord. The next is to do a caesarean section ASAP – get the baby out pronto!

First, the baby's head. Basically, the mum has to get on all fours, knees and elbows and then you insert your gloved hand into the vagina and physically keep the head away from the cervix and cord. Not exactly the most elegant of positions!

The regional centre was an hour away, once the ambulance was called and I wasn't too thrilled about making the journey given that the baby's heart rate was fluctuating so wildly. We would have to do it in our local hospital. My partner rang the regional obstetrician. Bugger, he was away. The surgeon was similarly uncontactable.

Nothing for it but I'll have to do it myself. One partner would do the anaesthetic; another partner would look after the baby, helped by another doctor from the other practice.

The ambulance arrives and we then loaded poor old Jane in her afore-mentioned inelegant position onto the trolley, cover her nether regions with a blanket and with my hand firmly wedged 'up there', proceed through the surgery waiting room past the astonished gaze of the day's few remaining patients!

I gave a somewhat ingratiating grin, feeling rather silly, whilst Jane had the great presence of mind to pull a blanket over her head!

Off to the hospital we went, all in a high state of adrenaline-fuelled excitement.

Straight into the operating theatre and onto the theatre table! Then one of the midwives took over my head duties and then we laid Jane on her back with the poor old midwife crouching under the table, keeping the head off the cord.

My anaesthetist partner was putting her to sleep, I was scrubbing and gowning and the other two doctors getting the neonatal cot ready. I was thinking that things were going quite smoothly for an emergency operation, late on a Friday afternoon.

Ooooh shit, the operation. I am the one that has to do it! There's no one else. A deep breath and then it all comes back, well most of it does anyway. A call from the surgeon, as I'm gowning and putting on my gloves. He is leaving the regional centre as we speak and will be there in half an hour. Meantime, we've still got to deliver this baby as quickly as possible.

Patient is asleep. I 'prep' the skin of the belly (wash down with iodine antiseptic) and then apply the drapes, which keep the operating field aseptic. The routine of doing this calms me further and I'm feeling not too bad at all. I pick up the scalpel and get to work. It's going well and it's all coming back to me.

A little while later, I notice that the anaesthetist is looking worried. He is fiddling with the anaesthetic machine dials, taking blood pressures and shining a light in Jane's eyes.

"What's wrong?" I ask

"Her pupil is fixed and dilated." (not a good sign and usually means brain damage!)

"Everything looks okay. I don't know what is wrong."

Then the penny dropped.

"Oh sorry, I forgot to tell you that she has a glass eye!"

"You BASTARD!" he says in a most uncharitable tone of voice.

After that, everything else was really rather anticlimactic.

The baby came out in good order and was ably looked after by the team. The surgeon arrived and helped me close up.

However, for a while afterwards when my partner passed me in the surgery corridor the word 'BASTARD' floated around *sotto voce*.

Paracetamol
Gentle to the Stomach

Paracetamol, or to give it its proper name acetaminophen, has been around with us for years. Easily obtainable at the supermarket and most of us have the odd half packet lurking in the cupboard somewhere.

It is an effective reliever of mild to moderate pain and is used for all ages, during pregnancy and for small children.

If used correctly and the recommended dosing schedules adhered to, it is safe and effective. Though, I must say that some children have had problems with it when given for a prolonged period of time, even at the recommended dose.

But, it has a dark side and is extremely dangerous when taken in overdose and frequently fatal. It is one of the major causes of liver failure in the western world.

The problem is that most of us think it is innocuous and 'safe'.

The lowest dose that I know of that has resulted in a fatality is eight grams (or 16 x 500 milligram tablets). As they are sold at supermarket checkouts in packets of anything up to 100 x 500 milligram tablets, the capacity for harm is immense.

I have seen paracetamol used for a 'para-suicide' where to make a statement, someone has taken a whole packet on a 'look what you made me do' basis. Only for the parents/friends to say, "It's okay. It's just Panadol." By the time that symptoms of liver failure manifest, it is too late and the situation is irretrievable. By that time also, usually the person involved had decided they didn't really want to kill themselves but again too late.

How does it wreck the liver, then?

Funnily enough, (though there is no humour in it) paracetamol is okay by itself but when it is metabolised in the liver, it is the breakdown products of that metabolism that does the damage and is highly toxic to the liver.

There is an antidote called N-acetyl Cysteine or NAC, which works by occupying the metabolic sites where the paracetamol is broken down in the liver cells. The infusion is given intravenously over a day or two and works by blocking the liver cells metabolising the paracetamol until it is excreted unchanged via the urine.

To work best, the NAC infusion should be commenced within a few hours of the paracetamol ingestion and certainly within 12 hours. It then continues for a number of days

The story I want to relate to you happened many years ago when I was an intern (first year after graduation) in one of the large metropolitan hospitals.

I was very lucky to be working for the professor of medicine, a lovely man, with a well-deserved stellar international reputation, on his medical unit.

I went down to the Emergency Department with the registrar (most senior of the 'junior' medical staff) to see someone who had been brought in by friends with a paracetamol overdose some 29 hours earlier.

His sad story was as follows:

Dan was a journalist in his thirties. He had been newly married for the last eight months.

The day before he had been brought to hospital, he had discovered that his new wife was having an affair with his best friend, whom had been the best man at their wedding.

Not surprisingly, he was totally overcome by finding this out and was so devastated that he decided to end it all and took 24 capsules of Panadiene Forte. These contain 500 milligrams of paracetamol plus 30 milligrams of codeine. These are used for strong pain and had been prescribed for Dan when he broke his leg some six months previously.

So, he had taken 12 grams of paracetamol and some 720 milligrams of codeine.

He went around to some friends' house in distress. They had a long talk and then put him to bed with a hot water bottle to 'sleep off' the codeine as he was very drowsy. The Panadol wasn't given another thought. It's safe, right?

He presented to the Emergency Department some 29 hours after taking the tablets, brought in by his friends as he was vomiting blood.

One of the things the liver produces are certain clotting factors that help the blood to clot naturally like when you cut yourself. In liver failure, these factors are not produced; so any slight abrasion or graze can bleed copiously. Many of you may be familiar with the anti-coagulant, Warfarin. That when used therapeutically, interferes with the production of the liver clotting factors to reduce coagulation of the blood in a controlled manner.

The degree of anti-coagulation is measured by something called the INR, which is the International Normalised Ratio. Most therapeutic users of Warfarin aim for an INR between 2 and 3, which crudely means that the blood is two to three times thinner (and less likely to clot) than normal. Spontaneous bleeding often will occur when the INR is above 4 or 5.

Dan's INR was 9!

We also measured the level of his liver enzymes in the blood. There is a base 'normal' level of these enzymes measurable in blood but this increases sharply if there is liver damage.

Dan's liver enzyme levels were approximately 100 times normal.

Dan was suffering severe liver damage and failure.

The sad thing was he seemed so normal – conversing normally and rationally. He seemed resigned to the breakdown of his marriage and even was talking about working overseas once the divorce came through.

I have never, ever forgotten the professor coming to see him in the ED. We had somewhat futilely started some IV NAC but it seemed a little late.

The professor spoke to him kindly for quite a while and then looked him straight in the eye and said, "I am terribly sorry to tell you, you are a dead man and there is nothing we can do for you."

(These were the days before good haemodialysis and transplants.)

How ghastly, especially as he appeared so normal and well and having a usual, normal conversation with us! Like we are now.

Dan came to our ward, completely shattered and his friends gathered around him and supported him. His wife was not in evidence.

Over the next several days, he slowly deteriorated. Within a few days his liver enzymes returned to 'normal' levels which was rightly (and sadly) interpreted to mean he had no functioning liver left.

He bled on occasions. He developed a 'liver flap' (when the arms are held in front of you, palms down, and the hands bent backwards, the hands 'flap' backwards and forwards – a sure sign of liver failure) and he eventually slipped into a coma.

The very distressing thing for all of us on the staff (not that the whole situation was distressing enough) was that he started to have epileptic type seizures with increasing frequency. Thankfully, Dan was comatose and had no awareness of this.

These could be controlled after a fashion with IV drugs but they increased in frequency and severity and required more and more medication to terminate them.

The ward staff were very upset and poor Dan was requiring almost one to one nursing which is difficult on most wards where the usual is one nurse to look after five to ten patients (more in these days of economic rationalism!).

Thankfully, the Intensive Care Unit (ICU), whom until then had stoutly resisted requests to transfer Dan to them, finally agreed to look after him, mainly because they had a one to one nursing capability.

Dan finally died some eleven days after presentation to the ED.

What a waste.

Like many of my medical experiences over the years, I have never forgotten Dan.

So when people ask me, "What are the most dangerous drugs available?" Paracetamol is fairly high toward the top of the list.

Be wary of it.

A Legend to the End and Beyond

This great man was, and still remains, an Australian legend. Not only for the motor sport, in which he excelled but most members of the public have heard of him and remember him fondly to this day.

He died near a small town in the hills east of our city on a spring day in the 2000s, during the running of the local Targa Rally in which he was competing.

I know this because I was there. Let me tell you what happened.

The Targa style of rally has come into its own in the last decade or so in Australia. It has been around, in some form or other, for many years in Europe.

Basically, it is similar in form to other types of rallying such as the World Rally Championship (WRC). Like the WRC, a Targa Rally has a driver and a co-driver competing in a vehicle and are timed driving a number of 'stages' during the event. A stage is a closed section of road, from which the general public and other vehicles are excluded and varies in length from just a few kilometres up to over fifty kilometres.

Unlike circuit racing, the cars do not directly race against and in contact with each other but rather drive each stage separated by several minutes. The competitor is timed over the stage and at the end of the event it is the crew with the lowest elapsed time for all stages that wins the event.

Targa differs from WRC a little in the classes of cars that enter. Besides having full specification rally cars, it also has speed-limited entries for historic cars, different classifications of car types (Example: Porsche, Mini) and anyone who would like to take part whose car passes muster. All entries must pass rigorous inspection, called 'scrutineering', before they are allowed to compete in the event.

For this event, most of the officials and many of the competitors stayed at a hotel on the eastern side of the city with good access to the event's stages in the nearby hills. Our friend was staying at that hotel.

The medical set-up was covered by an organisation run by a paramedic friend of mine. Each stage start had a MIV (Medical Intervention Vehicle) with a further one at the midpoint of the longer stages. Each MIV had a crew of at least two experienced paramedics with the odd doctor thrown in for good measure. The medical equipment carried in each MIV was exceptional, meeting and frequently exceeding, international requirements.

We also ran a roving MIV (called the ICV – Incident Control Vehicle), which had the same medical equipment as the others and was able to respond to any incident, assist in its management and generally back up the stage MIVs. My paramedic mate and I were in the ICV. He was the Chief Incident Controller and I was the Chief Medical Officer for the event.

The weather, which had been dry for the last few weeks, was showery which made the stage roads (all tarmac) a bit slippery.

The competition cars (fully set-up with proper race seats, five or six-point harness type seat belts and full roll cages) started first before the other classes of vehicles. Helmets are obligatory for all classes of the competition.

The first competition car was an all-wheel drive, full specification (called 'full spec' in the game) Subaru rally car driven by a very experienced (and nice) local guy.

The second car behind him was our friend with a well-known motor sports identity as his co-driver. Their car was a rear- wheel drive sports car, full spec, including roll cage. Rear-wheel drive vehicles always seem to me to be at a disadvantage when used for rallying, traction and road holding ability not being as good as an all-wheel drive vehicle.

Besides the vehicle, our friend also had some other potential problems. He had only just flown home from overseas less than 48 hours previously. In addition to being jet-lagged, he had been unable to do any pre-race reconnaissance ('recce') to view the stages and write 'pace notes' in concert with his co-driver.

Pace notes are compiled during 'recce', to be called out by the co-driver whilst they are driving each stage, enabling the driver to know what is coming up and adjust his speed and gear selection to the conditions ahead. It is said to add about 15% to the vehicle speed when done correctly.

Our friend had to rely on bought pace-notes. Whilst many competitors from out of town do that, none I know of come down to breakfast on the morning of the first day and inform us that he is going to win! It was said with his usual charming smile and self-deprecating chuckle but behind that we all knew there was a steely determination to succeed.

The first stage was on a very degraded road through a national park. The road had many poorly mended potholes and also many of the corners had bad cambers which tend to throw any car, especially one travelling faster than normal, all over the place.

The local rally expert was first on the road and said afterwards that it was a difficult drive. Our friend was next and despite the local guy's car being a full spec rally car, came out of the stage only seven seconds slower. I saw the in-car footage from our friend's sports car taken during that stage and it was frightening to see how 'all over the place', it was and how much he had to fight just to keep it on the road.

The next stage was further into the hills and a much longer one. It travelled through some bush areas, past a beautiful picnic area with a waterfall (often visited during weekends) and then through an area which had a lot of rural farm-lets. In this part of the stage, the roads were fast and straight, and the organisers had placed several hay-bale chicanes (basically a sharp double bend created to form an obstacle on the road) to slow the cars down and to stop them reaching Mach2!

The stage had been run once and the competition cars were gathering at the start to go through the stage again.

We were at the start in the ICV and stayed to see the first few cars, including our friend, commence it for the second time. The MIV and ambulance were also at the start.

We had just left to go to the start of the next stage and were about 500 metres up the road when we heard a garbled call on the radio that there had been an accident in the stage we had just left and would someone please, please send an ambulance straight away.

We turned around and drove to the start to see the MIV just departing into the stage. We received radio clearance to enter the stage and did so, soon overtaking the slower MIV.

The accident site was some 15 kilometres into the stage; so it took us a bit of time to get there. While the tendency is to rush and drive flat out to reach an accident or incident, the most important thing is to arrive in a condition to be able to render assistance, so circumspection is the order of the day.

I remember my mate saying to me, "I've got a bad feeling about this." I must say, I was feeling the same unease – vague but definite and increasing, as we got closer.

The accident site was at the end of a long straight bit of road, which had a slowing chicane some 400 metres before it.

There was a sharp downward sloping left hand bend with a large tree on the right-hand side. The road was wet and quite slippery, complicated by gravel thrown onto the road from the first passage through the stage.

The sports car was just beyond the tree with the driver's side door stoved in (the impact was between the 'A' pillar at the windscreen and the 'B' pillar between the front and the back seats – a notorious weak spot for impacts). Our friend, driving, had taken the full impact of the slide into the big tree right on his door.

He was sitting in his driver's seat, a slight smile on his face. His right forearm was obviously broken.

I always remember thinking, *Fuck, that's...and fuck, he's dead!*

And he was.

The co-driver was in the seat right next to him, conscious and apparently okay but complaining of a sore hip.

Apparently the last words our friend said to him were, "This is going to hurt."

We were able to help the co-driver out of the car on the passenger side and once the ambulance arrived, he was taken to hospital for a check-up. He had a minor hip injury and thankfully was discharged the next day and made a full recovery.

Our poor friend was still in the car and his legs were trapped by the roll cage which had been moved inward by the impact.

My mate, who is a very experienced senior ambulance paramedic, confirmed with me his death and was able to tape off the area. We used tarpaulins to shield the car from the nearby spectators.

We then settled down to wait for the police. This, gruesome as it sounds, was now a 'crime scene'.

The only light relief, if ever there could be at a time like this, was when the police arrived with three cars, sirens on and lights flashing, some 50 minutes later.

Two cars pulled up blocking the road with a heroic screech of brakes. The third car, coming up behind and having no place to go, wrenched their steering wheel over and ran up a nearby driveway, totally demolishing a farm gate in the process.

Black farce but no one felt like laughing.

The police wanted him to be removed from the car with minimal disruption to it. This meant trying to cut through the lateral aspect of the driver's side roll-cage, which had been heavily distorted and compressed in the impact.

Unfortunately, the cutters carried by our rescue service (great guys – similarly as devastated as we all were) weren't equal to the task, so we had to wait for the heavy rescue fire brigade team to come from some 50 kilometres away.

Once they arrived, they totally ignored the police and proceeded to open the car up like a sardine can – Great! Our boys could have done that an hour earlier.

By now, we were being buzzed by news helicopters, some of which landed in the paddocks nearby. The awful news had gotten out.

Thankfully, the police had enough resources to keep the media at a respectful distance from the site.

The final indignity was the arrival of the mortuary vehicle to take his body away. Thankfully, we had been able, finally, to get him out of the vehicle after the obligatory police photographs. We were able to lay him on a stretcher inside the second ambulance with some semblance of dignity and away from prying eyes.

He was then, at last, able to start the final journey home.

So, there it was – the death of a legend and a thoroughly nice person.

It affected us all deeply, which of course is nothing compared to what his poor family went through.

Could we have done anything different or better? Would it have made a difference if we could have got there more quickly?

Almost certainly not, as this was a non-survivable accident but I always will wonder.

Sadly, no matter who we are, no matter how well known we are, no matter what we do.

Not one of us is immune to the laws of physics.

Postscript

Well, for what it is worth, those are my stories.

I am drawing to the close of my working life and soon must face retirement, which I suspect will be a very mixed blessing.

It has been great. Mostly I have loved it, very occasionally disliked it, but always been grateful for being involved in peoples' lives.

I'll leave you with some sayings that you might find amusing, or not. To some extent they sum things up for me. I used to quote them to the medical students when I tutored some years ago

Thank you for getting to these penultimate pages. Well Done!

- To **cure**...sometimes; to **relieve**...often; and to **comfort**...always – Hippocrates
- More is missed by not looking than by not knowing.
- *Primum non nocere* – First do no harm
- "What makes me a caring person is the ability to laugh at the misfortunes of others." – Dame Edna.
- Learning medicine is like learning a foreign language. First you learn the vocabulary, then how to use it, then the slang and finally you arrive, when you think in that language. However, never forget that others not so proficient in that language, may not understand its nuances like you do. Adjust your vocabulary to suit the audience.
- In life and in medicine never forget the admonition – "Thy shalt not get up thyself."

- If someone says they don't make mistakes, they either don't see enough patients or they are lying. Or they just don't get it.
- No one is always totally on your side or totally against you.
- Medicine is a fine balance between adopting acceptable short cuts and not missing stuff.
- People are endlessly fascinating. "Once you have taken out two hundred lungs, it becomes all a bit *Ho-Hum*, the payoff is in the people you meet along the way." – Archie Simpson, Head of Cardio-Thoracic Surgery
- Everyone has a valid story to tell and life is full of heroism.
- You are the principal advocate for your patients.
- There is something to like in every patient, and something to dislike as well.
- If something like a new cure or pill seems too good to be true, it probably is.
- "Never be the first to adopt a new idea, or the last to abandon the old one." – Anon.
- "Put your finger in, so you don't put your foot in it." – George Pestell, Surgeon Extraordinaire about PR exams.
- "The examination of the abdomen includes testing the urine." – George Pestell
- Your degree gives you knowledge but only experience will give you competence and most importantly, perspective.
- Don't forget that if we all knew everything, we would be running the country.
- Never totally believe in, or totally, blindly adhere to any diagnosis; it may be wrong.
- There are very few instantaneous medical emergencies which will only give you time to act rather than think before acting.
- Patients and their relatives/friends indulge in magical thinking.

- All patients think that every headache is a brain tumour, every chest pain is a heart attack and every abdominal pain is appendicitis. Oh, and they all secretly believe that they have cancer!
- Some/a lot of patient perceptions about what is wrong with them come from women's magazines, Doctor Google and a friend of a friend, "who had something like that."
- "When arriving at an arrest, the first pulse to take is your own." – House of God
- "There is no body cavity that cannot be reached by a 14G needle and a good strong arm." – House of God
- "Life is like sewer, what you get out of it depends on what you put into it." – Tom Lehrer
- Patients appreciate humour but always be careful to laugh with the patient not at them.
- "Life is what happens to you while you are busy making other plans." – John Lennon
- "The more I see, the less I know for sure." – John Lennon
- No one comes out of the egg knowing anything.
- "Sweaty pilots live the longest." – My father, ex-Spitfire Pilot.
- "Dancing is a vertical expression of a horizontal desire." – Anon.
- Just when you think you've got the hang of it and you are rockinnnn', medicine has a habit of coming and giving you a swift kick in the bum.
- People who have a terminal illness don't really want to have yet another admission to hospital or test, however clever you think you are.
- Some doctors never touch their patients – always have occasion for the 'laying on of hands'.
- One of the lovely things about medicine is that you're allowed to care. We don't have to be all-macho. It's okay to cry sometimes but not all the time.
- Patients will generally tell you the truth, as they perceive it – unless they don't.

- Two phrases make my heart sink – "This will interest you, Doc!" and "I've never told anyone this before but…"
- Never be quick to criticise others especially colleagues. Remember, "There, but for the grace of God, go I."
- An alcoholic is someone that drinks more than their doctor.
- It's okay to be attracted to your patients. Just don't act on it.
- "Surgeons know nothing and do everything, physicians know everything and do nothing and pathologists know everything and do everything but a week too late." – Anon.
- "When you are up to your arse in alligators, it is hard to remember that the original objective was to drain the swamp." – Anon.
- At least 50% of what we now agree as medical gospel will be obsolete in ten years. The trouble is in working out which half.
- Every patient has something to teach you, all you have to do is listen.
- "The good thing about Alzheimer's disease, is that you keep on meeting new people!" – Dame Edna
- "The problem is that we all imagine that the game is designed so that you can win." – Anon.
- "Life wasn't meant to be easy." – Malcolm Fraser, ex-PM
- "Old-age isn't for wimps." – Anon.
- Ernest Hemingway was in conversation with F. Scott Fitzgerald Scott: "You know Ernest, the rich are different from us."
  Ernest: "Yes, they have more money!"
- Life isn't necessarily fair, but occasionally things work out okay.
- "No man is an island, entire of itself; every man is a piece of the continent, a part of the main, any man's death diminishes me, because I am involved in

mankind; and therefore, never send to know for whom the bell tolls; it tolls for thee." – John Donne
- Sometimes, despite your best efforts and use of the best equipment, the latest tests, and exemplary treatment, sometimes people just die. It's no one's 'fault' – it's just the way it is.

FIN.